The Campaign of Waterloo 1815

The Campaign of Waterloo 1815
A Political & Military History from the French perspective

Antoine Henri Jomini

The Campaign of Waterloo
1815
A Political & Military History from the
French perspective
by Antoine Henri Jomini

First published under the title
*The Political and Military History
of the Campaign of Waterloo*

Leonaur is an imprint
of Oakpast Ltd

Copyright in this form © 2010 Oakpast Ltd

ISBN: 978-0-85706-212-3(hardcover)
ISBN: 978-0-85706-211-6 (softcover)

http://www.leonaur.com

Publisher's Notes

In the interests of authenticity, the spellings, grammar and place names used have been retained from the original editions.

The opinions of the authors represent a view of events in which he was a participant related from his own perspective, as such the text is relevant as an historical document.

The views expressed in this book are not necessarily those of the publisher.

Contents

Preface	9
Campaign of 1815	11
Appendix	140

TO THE GRADUATES
OF
THE UNITED STATES MILITARY ACADEMY OF 1849
THIS TRANSLATION IS RESPECTFULLY INSCRIBED
BY THEIR CLASSMATE

Preface

This volume[1] was the last of a work, published some twelve years since; out as the manuscript of this campaign had unfortunately been mislaid, the editor was compelled to supply its place hastily and somewhat incompletely. Having, by an unforeseen event, recovered the original manuscript, I hasten to restore it in its integrity, with this difference, that I present it in my name, instead of causing the recital to be made by Napoleon. A powerful motive has induced me to act thus, and change the form employed in the rest of the work: it is, that the rapidity of the emperor's fall, and his exile, preventing him from procuring accurate information of what had occurred, not only in his army, but also in that of his adversaries, he had at St. Helena composed narratives, with which a disinterested historian could not entirely concur, so that it would have been necessary to make him utter things, of which he had judged altogether differently.

The censures that Napoleon has cast on Ney and Grouchy, and which these have returned with interest, have all, more or less, something specious in them. I have sought to be impartial in presenting them. Napoleon did not always give his orders in an irreproachable manner; these orders were not always well executed or properly interpreted, and his lieutenants knew not how to supply the deficiency in what they had received incompletely and vaguely. If I reproach Napoleon for any faults on the mornings of the 16th and 17th June, no one would suspect me, of wishing to cast the slightest cloud over his immense genius and glory, which, more loudly than any other, I have proclaimed in all my works. But the more laurels he has gathered, the less should his brow be adorned at the expense of his lieutenants.

---

1. General Jomini calls this, the 22nd chapter of his great work entitled *Vie Politique et Militaire de Napoleon*, though it is an unit in itself, and forms a complete summary of the campaign of 1815.—The Translator.

As regards his political course, it is not so easy to judge between his system and that of his detractors; in the first rank of these, figured all the ultra-liberal utopianists, professing the strange doctrine that power in a government and despotism are the same thing, and that, under pretence of producing liberalism, it was necessary, at any price, to curb the authority charged with directing the destinies of a nation It is evident that Napoleon thought otherwise, and the belief is admissible, that in principle he was right; perhaps he erred in exaggerating his doctrine of power; but it is very difficult to establish the just medium between nullity of power and the slightly arbitrary. The future will undoubtedly prove, that between two dangers, the emperor desired to choose the lesser, because the abasement of executive power, will always be the least equivocal signal of the decay of a nation; this decay, indeed, may not always be sudden, and sensible to the eyes of the vulgar, but will be the work of time, unless a powerful hand applies a prompt remedy in seizing the helm. As for the rest, my task is not to condemn or absolve: posterity will decide.

I will close by observing, that the ideas which prevail in this little work, being those recognized in all the acts of Napoleon, the Author found himself under the double necessity of adopting them and writing on the side of his interests, that is to say, by placing himself at the headquarters of the hero of this history, and not at that of his antagonists.   J.

1838.

Campaign of 1815

Filled for twenty years with the victories and gigantic enterprises of Napoleon, all Europe still gazed with astonishment at the sudden fall of an empire, whose power, till recently, menaced universal independence. It could not be conceived that six months had sufficed, for leading the allies from the Elbe to the Seine, and dictating to France the terrible treaties of Paris. The congress of all the powers, assembled at Vienna, was endeavouring to conciliate the numerous claims arriving from all parts, for shares of the spoils of this audacious conqueror who, two years previously, had dared to place one foot on Cadiz, the other on Moscow. The task was a difficult one, because this grand diplomatic act should accomplish the double purpose, of establishing the political equilibrium so severely shaken, and regulating for the future the European public right, utterly overthrown, by the storms of the revolution.

Fallen from the throne of the most powerful empire to the ridiculous sovereignty of the Isle of Elba, by reason of his abdication at Fontainbleau; separated from his wife and son in an almost humiliating manner, and for which history will one day justly reproach his enemies; Napoleon retired to Porto-Ferrajo, like Scipio in his retreat at Liternum, to some degree exiled, and more discontented at the desertion of his compatriots than the persecution of his adversaries.

Condemned by destiny to be but a passive spectator of the grand affairs of the world, which for fifteen years, he had directed by the ascendency of his genius, he yet bore within himself the secret presentiment of being called, soon or late, to reappear on the scene. He was too familiar with men and affairs, to feign ignorance of the full extent of the difficulties that would harass the Bourbons, in the governing of a country that had become changed since their departure, and felt profoundly humiliated by the disastrous circumstances that had brought them back. Napoleon was then well aware that, after the first infatuation occasioned by the general peace, immense interests and violent passions would come in conflict, so that the most energetic portion of the French nation would soon regret the termination of his reign and desire his return.

However, the uncertainty as to the time when this would take place, and his inability to give birth to the occasion, preventing him from forming his plans, the ex-emperor found comfort in the occupation of tracing the history of his life, and feeding the sacred flame in the bosoms of his partisans; while the progress of events was precipitated to such a point, that he was torn from his retreat much earlier than he anticipated.

Independent of the special advices he received from Queen Hortense and some faithful friends, the journals would have sufficiently instructed him in the state of affairs; for, notwithstanding the censure that weighed upon them, and notwithstanding their falsehoods, the divers passions they interpreted were visible to the least clear-sighted, and exposed the agitation that reigned throughout the kingdom.

Indeed, Louis XVIII. seemed at first to have perfectly appreciated the spirit of the age, in the conviction, that the majority of France desired to consolidate the results of the revolution. After twenty years of experience, this prince had concluded, that his party was too weak to resist the wishes of the immense majority of the middle classes, who, in a country stripped of aristocratic institutions, always finally dictated the law.[1] He felt that to maintain himself on the throne, it was necessary to reign with this majority, that is, with the interests of the revolution. *Henry IV. had said that Paris was well worth a mass,—Louis XVIII. thought that the crown of France was well worth a constitution.*

It was evident he could not govern through the ancient magistracy of the kingdom, of which not a vestige remained; nor was it with the

---

1. The opinion here expressed appears to have suggested to Napoleon his famous decrees from Lyons; but throughout the rest of his career, he seems to have laboured under the conviction, that if it be always well to act on the spirit of the masses, it is no less true, that majorities, or masses are rather disposed to be constrained and led, than to influence the direction of affairs. On great political questions votes should be weighed, not counted; because we know how ignorant the masses are upon such subjects, even among people who pretend to the highest civilization.

What can be expected from the political ability of the multitude, when in an assembly of four or five hundred deputies representing the notables of a country, it is nigh impossible to find fifty statesmen worthy the name—happy, indeed, if among them there be two or three politicians of the first order.

deceased states of Brittany, nor with those of Languedoc and Burgundy, that it would be possible to lead the France of 1814. It was necessary then, to recreate the entire machine on new bases, and in order not to submit to the revolutionary principles, it behooved the king to revive the work of the revolution by virtue of the divine right, upon which he founded his own; he, therefore, granted a charter.[2]

Many publicists have blamed Louis XVIII. for this important measure; and in judging it by the results it produced, we are constrained to admit that it accomplished its end badly. If it had been possible to seize the dictatorship with a vigorous hand, and govern through royal ordinances, it is incontestable that this had been the surest plan; but we are led to the belief that it was impracticable; the king had then but to decide, what governmental machine would be a proper substitute for that, which had just sunk under the blows of the allied powers. To re-establish the Assemblies or the states of the provinces, had been impossible, as we have just remarked; this had, moreover, clashed with too many long-lived interests and opinions to make the attempt possible. To substitute for the glorious and energetic empire of Napoleon, the absolute power of a *camarilla* of emigrants, was the dream of a visionary: if acted upon, the restoration had not lasted six months.

A woman, endowed with a superior mind when she spoke not of politics, has pretended, that the Bourbons ought to have taken the empire as they found it:—"*The bed was so well made*" she said, "*that they had but to lie in it*." This phrase of Madame de Stael, that met with so much success in the frivolous saloons of Paris, was but *nonsense*. How would the brother and successor of Louis XVI. have been able to recognize a Senate, that no people in Europe had acknowledged, after the conduct it had held towards its founder, and which, twice in ten years, had disposed of the throne?

As to the mute legislative body which has subjected the Emperor to so much censure, which had not dared to raise its voice, but at the

---

2. Many writers have affirmed that Louis XVIII. only concluded on giving a charter, at the reiterated instances of the Emperor Alexander. We are certain that the Russian Monarch did, indeed, give this advice to the French King at Compiegne; but it is not very probable that the charter of 1814 was the improvisation of a few days; everything leads to the presumption, that the opinions of the two sovereigns accorded on this occasion, and that the king had meditated on his course while in exile. However, his declaration from St. Ouen of the 2nd May, was followed by a compact, the provisions of which, agreed upon by Ferrand, Montesquieu and Dambray, were drawn up by Beugnot, and afterwards discussed with, a commission taken from among the authorities established by the Empire.

moment when a million of enemies were on the point of invading France, that is to say, at the moment when it was necessary to be silent and rally around the Chief of the State, and which had thus forced Napoleon to dissolve it;—it is certain, that it would have favoured the reestablishment of the royal authority better than the public tribune, which is ever ready to serve as an arena for the passions. But it is doubtful whether it would have been welcome to France. Moreover, the imperial institutions favoured the opinions of liberalism so little, that the leading doctrinaires of the senate, who had overthrown Napoleon, were eager to frame a charter to please themselves and to be imposed on the Bourbons; but Louis XVIII., decided in repelling this illegal act, should, according to the prevailing opinion, have promulgated another, reassuring the threatened interests.

The king had then but the choice of two courses: the first was to grant a charter, as he did; the second was to govern provisionally as dictator, while convoking a constitutional assembly to work in concert with his ministers, in the framing of a national compact which, sanctioned by the notables of France, would become irrevocable, and thus offer the double advantage of guaranteeing the interests of the throne, as well as those of the nation.

The first of these appeared to him the most prudent: first, because it was a voluntary concession, and did not implicate the recognition of the principle of national sovereignty, as the second would have done: Louis XVIII should, therefore oppose all his power to this principle, so specious in theory, as it might easily degenerate into a system of elective monarchy. Then, it was at least doubtful whether a well finished, well matured and very solid compact, could emanate from a constituent assembly, however restricted might be the number of its members. And if instead of an elective assembly, they were satisfied with a commission of forty or fifty members appointed by the provisional government, to which would be given the initiative in all the combinations of the compact, as was done after the 18th *Brumaire*, what guaranty had such authority presented? What power would a compact thus fabricated have had?

A king has always the right to establish institutions where none exist; but by what right would an assembly of fifty counsellors stripped of all legitimate power, impose a contract on royalty on the one side, and on the entire nation on the other, without submitting it, if not to the primary assemblies, at least to those of the notables specially nominated for this purpose by the country? But these two means were equally incompatible with the antecedents of the monarch and the true interests of his crown.[3]

The formality of submitting constitutions to the so-called popular voice, had actually become, since the revolution, a veritable comedy; for, from the famous ochlocratical constitution of Héraut de Séychelles in 1793, to the vote on the hereditary empire of 1815, every compact, however worthless, had received from two to three millions of votes:—all know of what value are the suffrages of the multitude in such matters, which the loftiest minds have such difficulty in understanding. The institutions of a great country should emanate from her chiefs, or, in their failing, from her notables; and if these are not capable of digesting them properly, the masses, far from improving them, would be incompetent to judge of their merits; as a consequence, would not be qualified to approve or reject them. If Napoleon had often recourse to it himself, it was because he held all his power by election, and was unable to give it any other basis.

Finally, the most important of all problems of high internal politics will always be, the proper determination of the kind and limits of a national intervention in monarchical institutions: the intervention of the country in the administration of ordinary affairs, is a point which it would be unreasonable to contest, though to render it useful, it must be wisely regulated; but with respect to fundamental laws above all, the initiative should not appertain to it; for if ever the deputies have the right to patch up charters and elect kings, then the monarchy becomes purely elective, and the fate of all states governed by this deplorable system, is sufficiently well known.

Louis XVIII. was too well convinced of these truths, not to deem a charter carefully drawn up by the counsellors of the throne as the wisest course, since he would equally avoid the danger to which he would be exposed in wishing to govern through royal ordinances, and the still more serious one, of abandoning the formation of this compact to an assembly of legislators, animated with the most hostile passions and doctrines.

Placed thus with the alternative, of disregarding all the traditions of a monarchy of fourteen centuries, by renouncing all the rights which constituted at once the splendour and the solidity of the throne, and in

---

3. I should state in this place, once for all, that the principles put forth in this volume, apply only to France and other so called constitutional monarchies; these forms of government would not suit all countries—no more suit the United States of America than Russia or Austria.

permitting troublesome laws to be imposed upon him, or of displeasing the nation, by acting according to his own good pleasure without consulting the country, Louis XVIII. sought to conciliate as much as possible the rights of the past and the opinions of the present, with a proper foresight to the future. He flattered himself to attain this end, by having his compact sanctioned by a commission, composed of an equal number of senators and members of the legislative body, chosen from those who had acquired an ephemeral popularity, by the loudest declamations against the imperial power. This measure with its good intention, served, however, but to introduce two or three deplorable amendments in the royal project, and did not prevent the utopianists of all shades from proclaiming the scandal, because, said they, the fundamental law being the work of a small number of the prince's favourites, can only be an act outrageous to the sovereignty of the people or the nation.

As the personal position of Napoleon placed him under the necessity of making frequent allusions to this sovereignty, which was really the only foundation of his right to exercise the supreme authority, it will not be out of place here to expose the manner in which all wise statesmen should regard it, and in which without doubt he also viewed it.[4]

Now-a-days, speculative politics have produced a veritable confusion of tongues, and to make myself properly understood, I feel the necessity of renewing here a species of profession of faith. In internal politics there are four things essentially different: theory and practice, men and systems. I will forbear from speaking of the different species of men thinking themselves political, and I will treat only of things, that is to say, of systems and doctrines. I will only observe, in passing, that the men called on to govern a state, are often under the necessity of adopting systems, which are not according to their principles: a legislator and a publicist are, on this account, in a more independent situation; but a prince, a chief of state, a prime minister, being obliged to put into operation the elements they have at their disposal, find themselves thus acting according to certain dogmas not their own; and this was especially Napoleon's case in 1815.

Some very ingenuous publicists have imagined in good faith, that

---

4. There are contradictions between these principles and many acts of Napoleon; but it must not be forgotten, that his position imposed upon him many deviations from his true principles, which otherwise, manifest themselves in all the grand measures of his government.

in point of political combinations, all was new under the sun since 1789. However, to my knowledge, there are but five forms of government that ever existed, and to which little has been added in our day; these are: absolute hereditary monarchy; hereditary monarchy limited by institutions; elective monarchy; aristocratic republic or oligarchy; lastly, democratic republic. I have been explicit on these different forms of government (chap. 7, vol. 2). Some have many advantages, mixed with some defects; others have grave defects, tempered by feeble advantages. I have described both.

When we attempt to give a government to a country, that finds itself momentarily deprived of the same through certain catastrophes, it is necessary to choose aright one of the five forms indicated. Whichever be our choice, we should be deeply impressed with the fact-that no nation is strong, puissant and formidable, without a government that is vigorous and respected at home.—That no government is capable of leading a people to high destinies, when the authority is humiliated by those, who should make it their duty to elevate it to the highest degree of consideration.—Finally, that liberty and order are impossible, without due respect for the princes, the chiefs, or the magistrates.

If it be acknowledged that in our day, republicanism would be an absurdity in a great European state, with old communities scarcely free from the swaddling clothes of feudalism; if monarchy be the only form that can be proposed, then a choice must be had between the elective and the hereditary, between the absolute and the limited.

Though I have already commented on the dangers of all elective governments, especially when applied to monarchy, I must recall here what I have said concerning it. In consulting appearances only, this system would undoubtedly seem the most founded in reason; still nothing is more opposed to the solidity, grandeur, and even the preservation of states, for it is little else than anarchy and civil war legally introduced into the country at the death of each king. The visionaries who extol it unceasingly, are unaware, that no elective monarchy would exist a century in the midst of powerful neighbours, jealous and interested in intervening at each succession to the throne, in order to excite a civil war, or cause the election of a king suited to their wishes. They forget that Poland perished, solely because she was an elective monarchy, *endowed with citizen-kings*; that Hungary and Bohemia have been swallowed up for the same reason.

We know what ruptures the federative and elective empire has produced in Germany. The Grand-dukes of Moscow, and the Arch-dukes of Austria, hereditary possessors of feeble provinces, have, on the contrary, founded the two most powerful monarchies of modern times, at the expense of the republics and elective monarchies by which they were surrounded. If France, when tired of the despotism of Louis XI., (which nevertheless gained her so much power,) had thought of seeking for a remedy in an elective government, she would have long ago been effaced from the map of Europe as a political power. The greatest service Napoleon has rendered her, is most certainly that of having abolished her elective government, to lead her back to wiser institutions.

It was after having recognized these incontestible facts, that all wise legislators adopted, from age to age, the principle of legitimacy, or the order of hereditary succession, as the true safeguard of monarchical states.[5] But, one fact that has been too much forgotten by our modern Solons is, that the principle was established much more for the interest of the state than for that of any one dynasty whatever; and that consequently, the slightest blow given to its fundamental laws would lead to great future disorders.

An elective monarchy not being then more suitable than a republic, there remains but to choose between an absolute hereditary monarchy and one limited by institutions: each has its good features as well as its inconveniences. If the prince was always a just, firm man, and a great statesman, or if deficient in either of these qualities, was always surrounded by honest and able ministers, an absolute monarchy would certainly be the government *par excellence*. If the chambers of a constitutional country were all composed of true statesmen, incorruptible and impartial, without vanity or ambition, without spirit of party or association, dreaming but of the country's grandeur and of respect for the dynasty; in one word, sacrificing but to one divinity, *the public good*, they might perhaps be able to dispute the palm with a wise absolute royalty, and offer the perfection of social institutions. But it is impossible to find such chambers in any country. Thus, every system having its inconveniences and its dangers, the aim and end of all fundamental law should be to diminish them as much as possible, and the institu-

---

5. The good is often confounded with the bad, legitimacy with absolute government; the liberals honour them with one and the same anathema, and nothing is more absurd, because, since the law of the country establishes hereditary monarchy, each one should be a legitimist as a matter of duty, which does not at all prevent his being a constitutionalist

tions that will permit the least to exist, will evidently be the best.

In order to compensate for the dangerous accidents which the exclusive principle of legitimacy and inheritance offers in sometimes leading bad princes to the throne, some have imagined a constitutional government, others the principle of national sovereignty; high-sounding terms, that often conceal many deceptions, and the meaning and application of which are not often well defined or well established. To this system some legislators of great foresight have preferred the divine right, seeing that all power having necessarily a source and origin, it was very necessary to ascribe one to royalty; but, if national sovereignty is cast aside as evidently dangerous, nothing is more rational than the recognition of royalty as coming from God, since his providence guides the destinies of nations as well as of individuals.

Between these two systems that appear reciprocally to exclude each other, there perhaps exists a middle course; undoubtedly sought for but not yet found, or at least it still remains unfixed. Little has resulted from this attempt, but an unconnected system, with which they have thought to reconcile the elective principle to the hereditary, by uniting them under the head of national sovereignty, a kind of bastard legitimacy, consisting of an order of succession without strength, as it would be actually revocable by a vote of the country more or less properly ascertained. Others, more bold, or less satisfied with this vague sovereignty, have believed it possible to appeal to that of the people as the most positive and most powerful.

These terms, sovereignty of the people and national sovereignty, have unfortunately been very often confounded, though they signify very different things. The sovereignty of the people or of the multitude, is an absurdity that no reasonable man can sustain, unless a totally different signification is given to it from that which it is generally supposed to have. If it is imagined that the multitude reigns because it nominates delegates direct, as it was pretended to establish under the national convention, a great mistake is committed, because the people never were less the sovereign than under this deplorable system. If classes of notables are created, and the right of choosing delegates conferred upon them, the people, no longer nominating their proxy, are then no longer the sovereign. Besides, did there ever exist a people truly capable of exercising even the most indirect sovereignty? This has never occurred even in the small cantons of Switzerland.

Under all constitutional monarchies, national sovereignty expresses, according to all reasonable statesmen, the sovereignty of three powers, that have authority to govern the affairs of the country: one only of these powers, then, is never but a fraction of the sovereignty. Now, a nation delegating but one of these powers, is not, properly speaking, sovereign, because if so, the power of its delegates would rule alone, and would annihilate the other two.

We see by this expose, that national sovereignty has not yet been generally well defined nor well understood. The intervention of a nation in the administration of public affairs, is not only a desirable fact, as has been already stated, but is a universal fact that exists even in absolute monarchies, as the sovereign cannot govern without being surrounded with men of merit designated by public opinion, and who, under some title or other, frame into ordinances the wishes of the nation, indicated by the provincial states or the municipal administrations. This intervention of the country in the management of affairs, is naturally clearer and stronger under a constitutional government, where there exists an elective chamber called to discuss and approve the laws; *but there is an immense distance between this intervention in affairs, and the sovereignty.* And it is very necessary that it should be so, for it would be a strange play upon words, to pretend to establish an hereditary monarchy side by side with a national sovereignty, so understood, that the nation being sovereign, her delegates would have the right to make and to destroy the government.

It is true, that after the grand political deluges that have occasionally engulfed some old, rotten, and powerless governments, or after the total extinction of some dynasty, it has been very necessary that the notables of a nation should provide for the rebuilding of the state, by confiding the reins to the prince judged most worthy and apt, or to him who had the most direct right. But this act of election being an exception to the fundamental principles of inheritance, and not being justifiable but under imperious circumstances, is far from constituting a sovereign right; it should be considered only as a revolution, and the compact resulting from it proclaiming the heirship to the throne, becomes by this fact a distinct reparation of the violation of the principle, and a positive abdication of this pretended right of national sovereignty. If it were otherwise, a monarchy would be only elective, as has been already stated.

It results from this, that in a hereditary monarchy, not absolute, but limited by fundamental laws, *the throne is the legitimate property of the dynasty, the same as that the portion of sovereignty that consists in taking part in the framing of laws, is the imprescriptible property of the nation.* The nation should then be powerless in disposing of the throne as long as there is an heir direct or indirect to it, as the throne cannot deprive the nation from participating in the administration of affairs; a concurrence that it exercises not only through an elective chamber, but also through a chamber of peers or senate chosen from the *notabilités* of the country, and which, although nominated by the king, would not the less represent an active and powerful fraction of the general interests of the country.

The equilibrium of, and the putting in practice these two portions of sovereignty, is the delicate problem that all wise statesmen should seek to reduce to a fundamental law. There are but few of our modern legislators who have properly comprehended this problem, or at least, who have given it a satisfactory solution.

If they have not perfectly understood national sovereignty, neither have they properly appreciated and defined divine right. The most ardent innovators have endeavoured to exhibit it as a right at once obscure and arbitrary, which in distant times, some sovereign families had arrogated to themselves, over the property of a country. Louis XIV. especially, in his strange instructions to his grandson, had in some manner given the weight of authority to this erroneous opinion. But far from its being an abuse sanctioned by time, the divine right had a more noble and more solemn origin, because it was indisputably the most sublime institution that legislators could devise, for giving to a state the stability which constitutes strength, power, and prosperity, and delivering it from civil discord, by having the throne protected from ambitious individuals.

It thus became an article of faith, among learned men through profound reasoning, and among the masses through tradition, not for the interest of one family. but for the very safety of the state and the greatest advantage to national power. Happy the people who are sufficiently wise to know how to enjoy the benefits of an advanced civilization, by appreciating the advantages of such an institution, and seeking to fulfil the duties it imposes.

After the English and French revolutions, the divine right was exposed to the attacks of that multitude of writers who thought themselves born to shape the destiny of nations. Even among statesmen of sufficient learning to discern all its merits, there were found some who considered its action insufficient for a society shaken to its foundation, and in which religious belief had given place to a spirit of scepticism and controversy that pretended to make everything pass through the crucible of philosophy. These bold writers thought that a right which latitudinarians and even all the intelligent classes called a precedent, a right, according to them, that lost itself 'mid the clouds of fanaticism, could not have as solid an origin as one proclaimed and consecrated by the interests of all, one, in a word, founded on the institutions judged to be indispensable by the most eminent men, and upheld by the experience of fifty centuries. In their opinion, the question, in point, was to draw up the fundamental law in such a manner as to place legitimacy under protection from all storms.

To this reasoning, not devoid of some justice, the defenders of the divine right answer, that human institutions being unstable by their nature, and sanctioned by men only, can of course be revoked by men, so that they would be necessarily subjected to all the storms of an elective monarchy, from which the divine right alone could entirely exempt them.

We have not decided here between the two systems of legitimacy, which will be equally indispensable according to the country where they are to be applied, and which at bottom rest on the same thought, because in either, the throne and the supreme power properly appertains by right to the family in the established order of succession; the only difference existing between them is, that in the latter the necessity of this order, that cannot be at all assailed, is recognized by human laws, which can be applied equally to an absolute as to a limited monarchy.

This human institution of legitimacy is the more admirable, as it has been necessarily sanctioned in its origin by the proudest families of a country, by those even who, having the chance of reaching the throne in their turn, would be supposed inimical to a stable institution that interdicted their ever having access to it. Well, by a very extraordinary conversion, those who have shown the greatest attachment to legitimacy, are the haughtiest families of England and France, while it has been the object of the sarcasm and hate of all demagogues who have nothing to gain by an elective system of monarchy.

Be that as it may, Louis XVIII. and his ministers, could with difficulty change of their own free will, the essence of this right, placed above mortal combinations, which had given fourteen centuries of continued existence to the monarchy of the Franks; they should naturally have made it the lever of the new public right, that dating from 1814, was to constitute for the future, that of the throne and of France, by binding them together in an indissoluble manner. All that could be demanded of them was, to establish forever, this alliance of divine inheritance with human institutions: the one deciding on the ownership of the crown, the other admitting and limiting at the same time, the rights of the nation, thus rendering this double basis unassailable, as well on the part of the throne as of its adversaries.

If the entire ancient nobility and all the members of the royal family had shared these sentiments, that were certainly entertained by the King personally, and his ministers, we must admit that the charter would have given satisfaction; because, if it imposed some slight trammels on monarchy, it shackled anarchy so much the more; but we should not ignore the fact that the successors of Louis XVIII. did not consider themselves at all bound by this contract, and claimed the divine right to the fullest extent, under the idea that it was attributed to them of old, especially under Louis XIV. Moreover, if the intimate counsellors of the King, Ferrand, Dambray, Montesquieu, Beugnot, had exhibited an enlarged sagacity in the framing and the discussion of this charter, the first two especially would have abolished from emigration, the exaggerated prejudices on the means of applying their doctrines to the French nation, usually little disposed to comprehend their abstractions; besides, the reactionary passions of some of these ministers and of other confidants of the monarch, were more dreadful even than their dogmas.

Their task was the more difficult from having to struggle against the Utopias of Benjamin Constant, Lanjuinais and Lafayette, and there was none, even to Beige Lanbrechts, appointed senator by Napoleon, who did not consider himself as well qualified as Louis XVIII. to give France a charter of his own fashioning. He deigned his consent to call this prince and his dynasty to the throne they had occupied for ten centuries, on condition that he should resume all the chains imposed by the National Assembly on Louis XVI. This flaming legist pushed his monomania so far, as to insert an article in his compact, prohibiting the king from making propositions under the form of laws, permitting him solely to pray the chambers for the passage of a law on a subject, upon which the prince would be satisfied in submitting an abstract. What perfect folly to put the base of the edifice at the summit, and the summit at the base, and which gave ample reason, why the King should refuse to such minds, the initiative of the compact.

After having demonstrated that the granted charter had a double necessity, I should remark that its arrangements were not faultless. As it was a sort of indissoluble contract, binding at the same time the throne and the nation, it should have been as brief as possible, and should have contained but one species of declaration of rights. Exception then can be taken, to its extending with too much complaisance over certain details of legislation, which it had been more proper to deliberate upon and modify afterwards with the aid of the chambers and the sanction of experience; the prerogatives conferred on the elective chamber were not so stipulated, that the equilibrium of the three powers so much desired, could never be broken by this last, and not become a vain word through its encroachments; by permitting an absolute liberty to the press, it left an opening to its misrule.

I am ever ready to avow, that this last fault was the work of the legislative commission associated in the discussion of the charter, and not an act of the king, who had wisely stipulated, that the laws upon this subject should have the power to prevent the often dangerous errors of the journals, which by exciting the worse passions would be itself capable of shaking the most strongly constituted governments. Finally, the most grave fault with which it can be charged is, that it was accompanied by circumstances and restrictions that caused its sincerity, and consequently, its duration, to be doubted.

If Louis XVIII. had not, with some reason, feared to establish grievous precedents in admitting dogmas, that might insensibly lead to the elective system, it is certain that he would have given more stability to his new edifice, by securing it at least the sanction of the new chambers if not of the country. It would have sufficed for this to have ordered a royal sitting, at which he had declared the compact obligatory on himself and his descendants, as well as on the nation and its deputies, each within the limits fixed by the charter. After which declaration, himself and all the members of his family, as well as all the deputies and peers, should have sworn to maintain in its integrity, a charter that was henceforth a contract binding on all, and the basis of an entirely new public right.

Far from acting with this frankness and this profound consciousness of the general interest of parties, they affected to permit the belief that they submitted to a necessity, but that this course would not be long followed. To this error the restoration added the no less grave one of changing the flag, and proscribing that which had been, during twenty years of triumphs, the pride of the present generation, instead of unreservedly adopting the national colours, which Louis XVI. and Louis XVIII. himself, had borne for two years. The white flag not only humiliated the army, but also became the emblem of a reactionary will that alarmed the best minds. Even Count Montlosier, whose pure royalty was well tested, protested, by his wise counsels, against an imprudence that placed the throne at the mercy of a banner. The king yielded to the excitations of his orthodox advisers, and believed he had accomplished sufficient in giving such liberal institutions, the principles of which, were far from obtaining the assent of the ultra-royalist party that surrounded him.

Be that as it may, Louis XVIII. hoped to be able, through this grand act, to bring together the Bourbons and the party that repulsed them, and render the revolutionists partisans of royalty, by maintaining their interests and admitting a portion of their system.

They imagined then, that there was but one heart and one mind in the entire nation; they affected to repeat it, but this was not true. There was, however, so much felicity in this combination, that under this *régime* France would have flourished in a few years, if parties would have reasoned: if pride, interest and the passions could have been annulled by some statute: lastly, if the errors we have just pointed out had not rekindled all the most opposite political passions. The king, by a dash of his pen, should have solved the problem struggled for, for twenty years, since he had established the new political doctrine in France, and caused it to be recognized without dispute by entire Europe. To succeed, it was only necessary for him to know how to be master at home; but this was the difficult point.

In fact, no chief magistrate was ever placed in a more vexatious position. Surrounded by twenty thousand emigrants who wanted situations, old imperial *employés* who wished to preserve theirs, Jacobins who also demanded a share of them, theorists who pretended to be alone capable of conducting a constitutional state, ancient royalists and a haughty clergy, who wished neither a constitution nor those charged with executing its requirements; Louis XVIII. had been an angel, a genius, to have succeeded in uniting the parties. This truth once acknowledged, he should, at least, have striven to fix insuperable bounds, and *walked through these dangers with a free and firm step.*

A prince who disposes of a thousand millions a year, besides all the employments in the administration and the army, eventually succeeds in everything, *when he has exclusively the initiative of the laws*, and knows how to employ wisdom and vigour by turns. To place the moderate royalists side by side with the constitutionalists and the statesmen moulded under the empire, to reject the ultras of all classes, to express his wishes haughtily and frankly, was the only course to be pursued;

perhaps it had not sufficed to consolidate a restoration, following immediately a foreign invasion and the military humiliation of the country; but at last, this was the only means of maintaining his position; vigour founded on justice, is the best subtlety of kings.

Louis XVIII. wished it too well done; he flattered the two factions too much, hoping to attach their chiefs to himself; he favoured Carnot and Fouché while protecting those who treated them as brigands; at the instigation of his counsellors, he promised the emigrants what the charter never allowed them. Instead of being the sole and vigorous chief of the state, he seemed but as the victim offered as a sacrifice to the animosity of both parties; *a secret power protected by his brother, and which pretended to more royalism than the king, had established itself at his very side in the palace of the Tuileries.* To increase his misfortune, authority was given to disreputable ministers, who were influenced by the coteries that disquieted the court. From that time there was nothing but inconsistency and contradiction in the system of government; words were never followed by deeds, as at heart they desired something different from what was promised in writing.

Louis XVIII. had given the charter to prevent any other from being thrust upon him; but it was evident that, the first moment passed, the orthodox royalists expected it to be withdrawn piece-meal, as the compact did not suit them. They openly proclaimed that this was but an act of transition between the revolution and legitimacy. The emigrants wanted an easy master, as was asked by the Spanish priest, one who would permit them to govern without contradiction. They saw in the return of the Bourbons, but a means of indemnifying themselves for their losses and recovering their privileges. They had caused their own ruin, and presented themselves as victims of their devotion to the royal family. They boldly asked if there was but one legitimacy, and if the rights of the nobility were not as sacred as those of the house of Bourbon.

To calm these pretensions, they promised to satisfy them in the course of time; but the charter was far from furnishing the means. In fact, the nobility was established, but it had neither prerogative nor power; it was not democratic, as it had exclusive pretensions; it was not aristocratic, as it did not constitute a body in the state, and to which the peerage itself was not exclusively reserved.

The clergy also preached against the charter, because they expected to reclaim their property and resume their ancient influence, which was positively impossible under the empire of the constitution. Rome also urged them in this course through an interest that had nothing in common with Christian morals, or with the well-being of the French church.

It was then evident that the entire structure reposed on insecure foundations. To consolidate it, required the strong will of Richelieu, joined to the principles of Henry IV. to put in practice what had been so wisely promised: *Union and oblivion*. Everything leads to the belief that this was the design of the princes; but as each one arrives, after protracted discords, nothing is thought of till interest and self-love have been extinguished or satisfied.

Instead of proceeding with this end in view, they did as in 1789, placed their self-love and interest at variance; those who had delivered Toulon to the English, appeared at the Tuileries side by side with those who had retaken it, and even dared to brave them with their raileries. The king should have sent them *en surveillance*, a hundred leagues from the capital.[6] To gain the general confidence, it was indispensable to expose, in a solemn proclamation, the principles of his government, and to assure their triumph in spite of all petty resistance.

Far from strengthening all acquired rights, and crashing all pretensions, the reverse was done, pretensions were caressed, and interests were injured. Already alarming reports, threatened all purchasers of national property with projects of restitution; pamphlets attributed to Chancellor Dambray, attacked the legality of the sales, and demonstrated the justice of restitution.

The soldiers of the empire were kept because feared, or rather because there were none others; and in reviewing them they affected to enhance the glory of their enemies. Crowds of emigrant or Vendean officers claimed, with perhaps some justice, the confirmation of their grades, thus encumbering the rolls of the army and staff, and depriving the officers, already too numerous for the army, reduced three-fourths, of all hopes of advancement. As a consequence, many military conspiracies had burst forth in the army through dissatisfaction.

Under the sway of circumstances such as these, no one could feel a confidence in the existing state of things, as they saw no point of support anywhere, and, at the head of affairs, neither power or will. Carnot, whose rough character was ever consistent, dared to weigh

---

[6]. We do not here mean that the king should prove ungrateful towards his faithful servitors. He ought to provide for and employ those who were moderate and wise; and exile from the court the over-excited and the firebrands who preached but reaction.

the weakness of this government in addressing the king; he afterwards published a memoir, in which, amid many truths, he feared not to apologize for the regicides, as well as for the sovereignty of the people. By the side of this memoir, the emigrants published pamphlets no less threatening.

They had not delayed till then, their conviction, that the establishment of a rostrum and the liberty of the press, were sad means for operating the fusion of parties, as these institutions would be more effectual in dividing the most united nation, than in rallying those, who were divided and irritated by the most violent revolution recorded in history. In fact, interest and self-love, wounded by the discourses from the tribune, as by the virulent polemics and personal attacks of the journals, revived all the passions, excited the hate that time and forgetfulness might have extinguished, and thus succeeded in creating factions even where none existed. It was indeed with this object—to allay all party feeling of resentment, and to merge all in the same interest for his empire, and not for the interest of his personal power, that Napoleon had established a censorship, whose unsatisfactory results were caused by deficient regulations. As the ministry of Louis XVIII. had felt, from the beginning, the necessity of establishing it over all works under twenty printed sheets, and especially over daily and periodical journals: this was one of the first laws submitted to the newly instituted chambers; and as it appeared to be contrary to the promises of the declaration of Saint Ouen and to the spirit of the modified charter, the liberals, republicans and doctrinaires raised incessant clamours: they shouted despotism! deception![7]

---

7. In the project of the charter emanating from the king's council, freedom of the press was declared, in conforming to the laws which would be restored for *preventing or restraining* its abuse; the legislative commission had objected to the word *preventing* and had obtained its erasure; the ministers afterwards decided that for *restraining* this abuse, it was necessary not to wait until the evil was without remedy and all its bad effects produced. Besides, all former censorship had been more or less illy-contrived. That of the empire confided solely to two or three mercenary censors, and extending to the most voluminous scientific works, was abused; years would be required to cull from the manuscripts accumulated there: the works in one volume, even the periodical reviews and pamphlets of ten sheets, should never be subjected but to good repressive laws clearly expressed. As regards the daily press, whose action is such as to be able to subvert the best constituted state, it should be subjected to a previous censorship, but instead of confiding this to complaisant clerks, it would be necessary, as I have stated in a previous volume, to institute *a special tribunal of irremovable judges*, that would both decide on offences committed by uncensured works and regulate the censorship of the daily press. (Continued next page.)

To these general causes of agitation, it is necessary still to add, the dissatisfaction which the onerous treaties entered into with foreigners had produced. All who bore a true French heart, all who had a spark of national pride and patriotism, were indignant at the ease with which the Count d'Artois had signed the order for restoring a hundred fortified places still occupied by French troops, before having even stipulated for any of the conditions for peace. The treaties of Paris traced out at the point of the sword with a rigor, undoubtedly justifiable as reprisals, but perhaps imprudent for the interest even of some of the powers that imposed them,—these treaties, I say, had left a deep-seated rancour in the hearts of all the partisans of the empire and revolution. Each one persuaded himself, right or wrong, that the Bourbons could have preserved at least a portion of Belgium and the line of the Rhine as far as Coblentz, as well as Savoy, if they had not been so eager to occupy the Tuileries. We do not intend to discuss here the validity of these censures, nor the possibility there may have existed on the part of the ministry of Louis XVIII. to obtain less harsh conditions; we only state the moral effect their eagerness had produced.

The result of so much conflict could not be long awaited. An absurd discourse of the minister Ferrand increased the irritation to the utmost, by classing all the French people in two categories: those who had followed the *right line*; that is to say, who had struggled in connection with the Bourbons or in la Vendee; and those who had pursued the *crooked line*, or who had admitted the Revolution and the Empire. A strange apostrophe to the entire nation, and a singular means of supporting a projected law, tending to the restitution of all the property of emigrants, not disposed of. Henceforth the parties, daily, appeared more hostile, and tin's shock might yet render Napoleon once more the arbiter of the destinies of France.

If the state of affairs in this country were of a nature to inspire him with the hope and the desire of returning, he was not the less stimulated by the intelligence of what was being enacted at the Congress of Vienna, where the division of the spoils had led to great dissensions. Already, were Austria, France and England bound by eventual treaties, to guarantee Saxony against the pretensions of Prussia backed by Russia, so that the not-over-satisfied sovereigns of these two countries, spoke of returning to their capitals that demanded their presence.

This was the only mode admissible in France, where the press has become a power sufficiently formidable to require particular judges, impartial by their position and capable of appreciating the good as well as the bad.

Their reported departure was fixed for the 5th March.

As a compensation for the support that the Bourbons promised to Austria and England, they demanded the expulsion of Murat from the throne of Naples, to be replaced by that branch of their family that formerly reigned there; a very natural step, truly, as it was a means of leading the peninsular to the interest of France. Besides, the venal and interested heart of Talleyrand attached a double importance to this project; since, to secure the preservation of his principality of Benevento and the revenues attached thereto, it behooved him to have it recognized by the legitimate government of the two Sicilies, to the restoration of which he inserted this condition. The Bourbons proposed to take upon themselves the expulsion of Murat, and with this object the assembling of troops in Dauphiny was taking place.

From another quarter Napoleon was timely informed that the ministers of Louis XVIII. were proposing to the Congress his removal from Elba, to exile him to another hemisphere; this was a gratuitous violation of the treaty of Fontainbleau, as up to this time he was chargeable with nothing that could provoke the anger of the sovereigns.[8]

Unable to resist such an attempt, because of his limited means of defence, and determined not to await the event, Napoleon conceived the audacious design of remounting the French throne. Though his forces consisted but of a thousand soldiers, they were, nevertheless, superior to those of the Bourbons, allied, as he was, to the honour of the country, which sometimes slumbers, but never dies in the heart of a war-like nation. Full of confidence in this support, he passed in review the small band, which was to second him in so hazardous an enterprise. These soldiers were ill equipped, but their martial forms denoted intrepid spirits. The preparations were not long, as these brave men carried nothing but their swords. Favoured by the fortuitous absence of the English commissioner and the vessels that watched over the Island of Elba, the small flotilla that bore them, met with no accident, and crossed over in three days. Napoleon again beheld the coast of France at Cannes on the 1st of March, near the very shore of Fréjus where he had landed fifteen years before, on his return from Egypt.

---

8. The French government did not pay the two millions granted annually by the treaty of Fontainbleau, and, it is said, inserted the condition that Bonaparte should be exiled out of Europe. Napoleon was informed of this fact by the Empress Maria-Louisa; and this circumstance, together with the false report of the dissolution of the Congress of Vienna, decided his return.

Fortune seemed as then to smile upon him, as he returned to this land, again to unfurl her standards, and restore her independence.

The landing was effected without opposition, but in finding himself once more on the soil of France, Napoleon must have experienced the liveliest emotions, for the nature of this enterprise might hold in reserve for him a most deplorable end. It appeared difficult to form a well digested plan, because of the want of information sufficiently detailed on the state of affairs in the south, all knowledge being gathered from the reports of prejudiced agents; he must have been satisfied with deciding on a course answering to the most probable case.

One of the first steps taken, to secure Antibe, failed completely, as General Corsin, who commanded, refused to receive the imperial troops. This first check seemed to augur badly, and it was the more grievous, being the act of a captain of the guard, who had taken the responsibility of trying this plan without orders. On the other hand, Toulon and Marseilles were not too well disposed. However, as it was important to strike with promptness, Napoleon was not long doubtful as to the course to be pursued, because a *point d'appui* in the interior was indispensable, and Grenoble was the nearest stronghold. He therefore marched upon this city as speedily as possible, the success of the enterprise depending on its occupation. The slender column that he called his army, arrived after having travelled eighty-four leagues in six days.

The welcome received from the population on the route, responded to his wishes, and doubled his chances of success, as he was satisfied that the portion of the people who were not corrupted by passion or interest, preserved a manly character, that the national humiliation had wounded. Reaching Vizille on the 6th of March, Napoleon at last met the first body of troops sent to oppose him, and who refused to parley with his officers. Aware that everything depended on the first *rencontre*, and accustomed to resolve with rapidity and decision, he fearlessly advanced to meet them, his breast laid bare, confident that they would not fire upon him. They were deeply affected by this act of recklessness and confidence; far from seeing in him an audacious promoter of civil war, as he was described, they recognized but their emperor marching at the head of his old warriors, who had so often led them on the road to victory; their hesitation was not of long duration. This was a detachment of the Fifth Regiment of Infantry, soon followed by the entire Seventh, under Labédoyère, who voluntarily hurried to his presence. The people and the soldiers having received him with similar exclamations of joy, Grenoble opened her gates, and he advanced upon Lyons with five thousand men.

At the news of his landing, the Bourbons, though struck with astonishment, yet flattered themselves with resistance. They put a price upon his head, and ordered him to be hunted down as an adventurer who, by force of arms, was attempting the well-being of the State. The Count d'Artois departed for Lyons with Macdonald; the Duke d'Angoulême, who was at Bordeaux, hastened into Languedoc, to establish the centre of a royal authority at Toulouse; Ney, summoned to Paris, was sent to the East; finally, an extra session of the chambers was called in all haste.

Some have even pretended that the most fiery of the ministers of the restoration, M. de Blacas, wished to have recourse to a surer means than that of the sword, and charged a man named B—— to assassinate the emperor.[9] Though an individual of this name has boasted, in a pamphlet, of having accepted this mission, we prefer suspecting this miserable man of madness, to giving credit to such an assertion. However, Napoleon affected the greatest tranquillity, feeling that he had glory and France on his side.

On the 10th March, and at the gates of Lyons, the royal troops were no sooner in the presence of his own, than they mingled with and embraced each other with cries of *Vive l'Empereur*. Macdonald barely escaped, and the Count d'Artois had just time to take post and return to Paris.

The Lyonese received the happy conqueror with still more enthusiasm than on his return from Marengo. This welcome, that deeply moved him, was an apology for his enterprise, and at once redoubled his courage and confidence in the future.

Although quite certain of the reception awaiting him at the capital, Napoleon issued many decrees at Lyons tending to affect public opinion. The greatest censures cast upon him by the ambitious party of the *tiers-état*, were for having re-established the nobility, enchained the press, and rendered the tribune mute. Notwithstanding he had acted only for the interest of public tranquillity, and in consequence of the grave circumstances under which an unexampled revolution had placed the country, he did not hesitate in retracing his steps, proclaiming the abolition of all privileged nobility, promising to govern conjointly with the deputies of the nation, and decreeing the re-estab-

---

9. See the pamphlet published by Moronval, *quai des Augustins*, in 1816, in which this. B—— gives an account of his exploits.

lishment of the liberty of the press.[10]

The two chambers which Louis XVIII. had conferred on France, found generally more partisans than the mute legislative body instituted in the year 8. Athenians in more than one point of resemblance, the French wished, at any price, to shine in the tribune, not dreaming that Demosthenes' are rare, and that for one statesman, a hundred ambitious, indifferent as well as interested declaimers, are found. Napoleon appreciated the advantages of the tribune, but was always aware of its disadvantages and dangers, and must have had at heart that France should enjoy the one without falling into the other. He however sacrificed his principles to the spirit of the age, well convinced that after the storm, they would feel the necessity of modifying anew, institutions that suited neither every circumstance nor every people; but the elements of which it is, however, proper that an enlightened nation should preserve, to be put into action, when a weak and incapable government or a dangerous minority set adrift the vessel of state.[11]

It would have been very remarkable, had Napoleon been able to forget the unheard of advantages that legitimacy gives, and the extreme facility with which Louis XVIII. had installed himself in his place in 1814; but being unable to invoke this principle in favour of his return, he was forced to oppose it with the principle of national sovereignty through its whole extent, as the best means of flattering the opinion. Persuaded, also, that in order to act sensibly on the impressible spirit of the French, it was necessary to refrain from following in the usual routine of the assemblies, with which the country had

---

10. The re-establishment of the unlimited liberty of the daily press was an error of which Napoleon became the first victim. The periodical press and works, may be exempt from censure, but the daily journals cannot be with impunity, at least during political storms.

11. This phrase will perhaps be thought ambiguous and little conclusive. It should be thus interpreted. Napoleon was convinced that the government with two chambers and a public tribune, offered real advantages in peaceable times, *when the wheels of government are well established by wise fundamental laws*, and especially when there exists but one interest, that of the state, closely bound to that of its chief, or, as well, under a feeble government whose chief is himself little capable of piloting the vessel of state. But he thought that after a revolution that has divided the nation into two hostile masses, when great interests, both injured and acquired, are *aux prises*, when there exists one government *de facto* and another *de jure* supported by foreigners, to deliver elements so combustible to public discussion, was to expose himself to inevitable troubles. This opinion can be shared with him without, as a consequence, being an apostle of despotism. I say farther, no one can think otherwise and be a statesman.

been disgusted, under every denomination, from that of the notables to the factious Senate he had dethroned, Napoleon conceived the idea of reuniting all the electors, not in their departments for the election of deputies, but at Paris, to form, under the solemn title of the Assembly of the *Champ de Mai*, an actual reunion of all the national *notabilités*, who would nominate commissioners to consult with him in the reconstruction of the State on future immovable bases.

This august assembly which would recall to mind the epoch when the Franks themselves raised their kings on the shield, also recalled the first federation of 1790, which, from its having been followed by the bloodiest catastrophes, was not the less one of the most imposing ceremonies to which history points. This Assembly of the *Champ de Mai* would charm, because of ancient and illustrious souvenirs; it would offer, he thought, a striking contrast to the manner in which the Bourbons had imposed a charter on the French, wounding the pride of the constitutional party, while the emperor strove to flatter the nation by affecting to render homage to her rights and her notables, with whom he was to confer respecting the new institutions to be given to the empire, for securing her internal happiness, consolidating her glory, and protecting her institutions from factions.

Napoleon did not entirely conceal from himself the danger that might someday result from such a precedent and the embarrassments under which his successors would labour, to whom he would bequeath all the vicissitudes of an elective monarchy. But having nothing upon which to act but the elective principle, it behooved him to make use of it for drawing together the greatest possible party, against the legitimacy of his enemies and the foolish pretensions of the Jacobins. Besides, he understood very well how, in time, to render all possible aid to the principle of hereditary succession; because this principle forming in fact the basis of the new public right, to secure its maintenance would be included in his duties.

Preceded by these memorable decrees, Napoleon continued his advance upon Châlons, where he was joined by the troops that Key had at first assembled with the intention to combat him. This marshal was no statesman, and the sum of his political creed consisted in not causing civil war for private interests. This was the motive that guided him at Fontainbleau, when he contributed to promoting the first abdication. *Nothing for one man—all for France* was his motto; a very respectable dogma, apparently, but which, when pushed too far, might cause the commission of grave errors, and lead to the forgetfulness of the most sacred duties.

At the report of the Emperor's return, Ney at first only saw the injury he had done him at Fontainbleau, and the dangers of a civil war with which his return menaced the country. He accepted in good faith the mission to repulse him by force of arms, and even gave vent to imprudent and improper threats against his ancient chief. But soon convinced, in his journey through Burgundy and Franche-Comté, of the unanimity of feeling among the people, and his very soldiers, who raised the national colours in his presence, and influenced by two officers who had been secretly sent him from Lyons, to guaranty to him oblivion of the past, the marshal repented of his first resolution, and trembled at the idea of giving the signal for civil war which he detested.

Placed in the same alternative as Marlborough between James II. and William, he did not hesitate to throw himself in the ranks he had rendered illustrious by so many brilliant feats of arms. He acted by impulse, and yielded to the idea that governed him, without reflecting that he offended against sacred propriety, which he could have easily avoided by retiring to Besançon until the entrance of Napoleon into the capital.

The contrast between his proclamation from Lonsle-Saulnier, and his promises to Louis XVIII., will remain an unfortunate stain in the history of his glorious career, because it gives a false idea of his character, by offering all the appearances of premeditated treason, of which he was incapable.

After his junction, nothing could arrest the happy conqueror, who pursued his triumphal march at the head of ten thousand men. He left to his adversaries but the resource of a camp, hastily assembled at Melun; but the soldiers of this camp, brothers to those of Grenoble, Lyons and Châlons, were more disposed to join their eagles than oppose them.

Stupefied by the rapidity of his progress, the royal government knew not where to show front; it would be difficult to picture the agitation and confusion that reigned at the palace of the Tuileries, as well as in Paris. Louis XVIII. had alone preserved that calm and that resignation that had never abandoned him. Yielding however to the unreasonableness of those around him, he permitted himself to adopt the most opposite resolutions. On the one side, he threw himself into the arms of *publicistes doctrinaires*, and confided to Benjamin Constant the drafting of proclamations that were to gain him the confidence and love of the French. He placed himself under the aegis of the national guards, and of the partisans of revolutions, while on the other hand he appealed to all the loyal royalists, and to the fidelity of the military, whom he had so seriously injured. Fouché was at one time at the point of being sent for at the palace and consulted, then they decided to arrest him; but the crafty sycophant decamped from his hotel in time, and found refuge in that of Queen Hortense, which he reached through a garden.

A few changes in the ministry; the police entrusted to Bourienne, who, from being Napoleon's confidential secretary and his friend from infancy, had become his open enemy; caresses and promises to all parties; appeals to the national guards and the royal volunteers; such were the sad measures with which Messrs, de Blacas, Ferrand, and Dambray counted upon frightening or capturing the conqueror of so many nations.

The chambers that had been so suddenly convoked, succeeded only in giving to the world the spectacle of nought from a deliberative assembly in presence of a real danger, and proved to entire Europe that the time when senators awaited death in their seats, had passed away forever. Moreover, this meeting resulted but in allowing some orators the pleasure of repeating the declamations inserted by Benjamin Constant in the *Journal des Débats* against the imperial despotism, in furnishing the ministry a pretext for avowing that errors had been committed; lastly, in giving the king an opportunity for appearing with solemnity before the chambers, accompanied by his brother and nephew, in order to take the oath of fidelity to the charter, which had been in better taste at the time of its promulgation; an oath, which on the part of the Count d'Artois, was ever suspected of little sincerity.

Two days after this sentimental but tardy homily, the troops of the camp of Melun went over *en masse* to those of the Emperor, who the next day, March 20th, made his *entrée* at the Tuileries. The Bourbons had but time to take shelter in Belgium; the Duke d'Angoulême alone, skirmished a few days in the South. Never had such an apparently reckless enterprise cost less in its execution. As an explanation, some have pretended that it was conformable to general opinion, which renders all things easy when floating with it. If the principle is true, its application in this case is at least doubtful; because, if we reflect on the state of opinion at the time of Napoleon's first abdication, the belief is permissible, that France was much divided in feeling towards him, and that the number of his enemies equalled that of his partisans.

In fact the former composed the most energetic portion of the nation. Besides, if it is certain that popular opinion be the most powerful of levers and supports, it is also necessary to keep in mind that it is no less fickle in its nature than difficult to establish, and that it is much more profitable to be its arbiter and director than be led a slave in its train; finally, if it be prudent at times to submit to its demands, it is well at a later period to get the mastery of it.

Be that as it may, this astounding revolution was terminated in twenty days without costing a single drop of blood; France had changed her aspect, the nation restored to herself, recovered her pride; she was free from the yoke imposed by strangers, having accomplished the greatest act of free-will of which a people are susceptible. The grandeur of the enterprise effaced the recollection of defeat, and Napoleon was again the man of her choice.

While awaiting the definitive institutions he had promised the country, the Emperor's first care was naturally to organize a temporary administration, and to place capable men in charge of the different offices.—That of war was given to Davoust, of the navy to Descrès, of finance to Gaudin: the portfolio of foreign affairs was restored to Caulincourt, whose pacific dispositions were known to the allies; Cambacéres accepted the seals after reiterated instances; Fouché took the ministry of the police, which was his element. Lastly, Napoleon confided that of the interior to that haughty republican, Carnot, who had refused to award him the Empire, in 1804, and who accepted the title of Count from that very Empire in 1811.

The choice of these two old adepts of Jacobinism, was at once, a pledge the Emperor intended giving to the public, against the errors of his so-called despotism, and a means of uniting in his defence that energetic portion of the people who served under their banners. He thoroughly appreciated the compass of Carnot's military genius, who, after having by instinct ordered certain passable operations in 1793 and 1794, had ordered very defective ones in 1796. But he had an energetic will and supported popular Utopias; he might be very useful in the ministry of the interior, to which appertained the duty of exciting the masses for the national defence, and organizing them accordingly. His character though much extolled, was impressed with a kind of probity and uprightness that had survived the revolutionary turmoils; this character, joined to talents for defending the country, we will admit, had made him a modern Cato in the eyes of the multitude: they thought, and with truth, that he would never be a servile agent of the imperial will; but they knew not how much good his inflexibility and his inclination to opposition might prevent.

As to Fouché, his character for intrigue is so well known that I can dispense with enlarging upon it. This man, who had a vast mind, though often false, considered cunning and actions of a *roué*, as the true genius for affairs. His great experience, while demonstrating to him the emptiness of the Utopias of demagogues, had not however succeeded in eradicating his doctrinaire ideas of 1791. He wanted strength in the administrative measures of the government, without comprehending that before everything else, this was necessary in the institutions.

Napoleon knew Fouché too well to confide in him; but if the latter treasured any resentment for the honourable exile the Emperor had imposed upon him in 1810, he had also to dread the Bourbons, who wished him arrested four days previous to his entrance into Paris, and who had great wrongs to complain of against him. A man of such a stamp, who had been stranger to no plot since 1792, who had planned, protected, or baffled them, could not stand with folded arms 'midst the grand conflict that was brewing. They had to resolve on using him by flattering his ambition, or placing him where he could do no injury. To confine him at Vincennes, or exile him without trial, would have caused much scandal at a time when they loudly exclaimed against arbitrary power. Napoleon preferred to employ him at all hazards, and paid dearly for this error. The numerous and audacious dependants who were grouped about these two ex-conventionals, and those ranged under the banners of Lafayette, Lanjuinais, and Benjamin Constant, signalized but too well the rude assaults which the new chief of the government would have to sustain unless he bound them to his cause. Experience had not as yet shown that they were no less dangerous as friends than as enemies.

Having thus attended to the formation of his cabinet, Napoleon felt it incumbent upon him to turn his attention towards Europe: the great Captain had refused the peace offered him at Châtillon, with the boundaries of 1792, because he then found himself on the throne of France, and it would have been too much condescension; but nothing prevented him from accepting the one imposed on the Bourbons, because he came from the Isle of Elba, and the responsibility did not weigh much upon him, neither in the eyes of France, nor in the eyes of posterity. While forewarning Murat of his departure, the Emperor had charged him to dispatch a courier to Vienna, bearing his pledge to adhere to the treaties of Paris, with the promise to confine his exertions to the internal happiness of France.

Unfortunately he had not a man of sufficient skill about him whom he might send to the Emperor Alexander, to demonstrate to this prince how much English rivalry would one day bear upon him, and how much value Russia should attach to the fact that France had a strong and national government, inimical to England. As his ancient projects on the Vistula, could not again recur, and as from this time no rivalry ought to exist between the two countries., it would be very difficult to affirm what effect such a mission would have produced on the mind of this monarch; but unfortunately this attempt could not be made.

In either case it was natural to believe that the positive assurances given by Napoleon to the sovereigns, would have had their due effect; because Europe, astounded by his return, and by the energy of the French people, must have dreaded the repetition of the scenes of the revolution, by provoking the display of all the resources of propagandism. The success of this step would not have been doubtful, if the Congress had been dissolved, as was assured him, and if the Emperor had treated with the cabinets singly.[12]

But the sovereigns being present, their pride was roused; their interests, divided since the fall of the Empire, to a degree difficult to reconcile through negotiations, could in twenty-four hours be rallied with a common object, that of consolidating the division of the rich spoils which Napoleon's return had rendered problematical. It was useless to protest his adhesion to the treaties, they wished to believe nothing; the coalition was renewed even before his protestations reached Vienna. All the governments that had placed arms in the hands of their people, only saw in his return a military revolt, capable of reviving the deplorable epochs when the Roman legions disposed of the Empire at the will of their ambitious commanders; each of the sovereigns was fearful then, right or wrong, of seeing his throne exposed to the same dangers.

Moreover, Austria trembled lest Italy should be snatched from her, forgetting altogether the ties which the events of 1814 had broken asunder. Russia, convinced that she could not preserve "Warsaw, but

---

12. This was written in 1828, and the conduct of Europe in 1830, proves the truth of the assertion. Napoleon departed, believing in the truth of the articles written from Vienna by Latour Dupin, and inserted in the *Journal des Débats*. They announced the departure of the king of Prussia and the Emperor Alexander as certain.

in allying with her most natural rivals, sacrificed everything to this end. Prussia, that solicited at Vienna for the dependency of Saxony, accepted the other enlargements that were assured her, fearful of not getting either. England, led by inferior men, thought she foresaw a second time the imperial eagles floating at Boulogne, at Antwerp, and in Egypt, and lavished her subsidies to escape an imaginary danger, or at least, one very exaggerated.

Thus were all interests at variance with the existence of Napoleon. The declaration of the 13th March, which placed him in a certain manner without the pale of the laws of nations, sufficiently proves the fears he inspired. If to all these motives, we add the dread felt by Talleyrand of this return, the result of which was to sequestrate the ten millions of *bernois* funds he had in England, at the same time that his fortune would be compromised in France through his banishment, the violence of this famous declaration will be easily understood, as the wording of the same has been generally attributed to him.

In order to appease the powers, it would have been necessary for the Emperor to have time to ensure the Duchy of Warsaw to Russia, and the cession of Italy to Austria. It would perhaps have been attended with success, had the negotiations been transferred singly to St. Petersburg and Vienna. But the declaration of the 13 March, made at an European Congress, left but little hope of success to these propositions for preserving peace.

However, Napoleon at first thought that this declaration had been prompted by the desire to second the resistance which the Bourbons might oppose to him, as well as by an exaggerated distrust of his ulterior projects towards Europe. Nothing was more natural than that the monarchs whose victories had reseated Louis XVIII. upon his throne, should seek to maintain him there; but when the prince had been so easily forced to another emigration, the question changed its aspect. The Emperor had then reason to flatter himself that the cabinets would retrace their steps, when informed of the rapidity of his triumph, and of the unheard of success of his enterprise, as well as of his pacific intentions. Unfortunately, the treaty of alliance, *offensive* and *defensive*, signed the 25th March between the great powers, very soon destroyed this illusion.[13]

---

13. Some rather credulous publicists have attributed an essential part in these important resolutions of Congress, to the intrigues of Fauche Borel, a secret agent of the Bourbons; it requires an astonishing quantity of simplicity to believe that the cabinets of the great powers could listen to the insinuations of such agents, in order to regulate their conduct under such grave and important circumstances.

We are not certain that this resolution of the sovereigns was really suggested by the general interest of thrones, and that under this supposition it was best because more expedient. The dynasty of Napoleon had been gloriously inaugurated by victory, into the number of those who reigned in Europe, and his alliance with the daughter of the Caesars had doubly enfeoffed him. Besides, it had perhaps been wiser to have left him on the throne, than have him replaced by a government which being imposed through violence, could with difficulty secure the repose of France and of Europe.

It can scarcely be credited, that the fear of beholding in this country the triumph of the elective principle and that of national sovereignty, a sufficient motive for so extraordinary a coalition; because this solutive principle could not gain ground in Europe through its partial application in any one country whatever; and if the ambition of France was dreaded, nothing better could be done, than endowing her with future ruptures by permitting her this elective government. Besides, when a principle is considered fatal to states, it should not be resisted with cannon, but by sage discussions, with experience and in time. Napoleon, by accepting the treaties of Paris, and maintained on his throne, would have strengthened the governments generally, suppressed revolutionary ideas and averted the crisis which has well nigh overthrown Europe two or three times since his fall; the volcano that still smokes more threateningly than we imagine, had been extinct or smothered for an indefinite period, and the European equilibrium had been more firmly re-established.

In fact, it was difficult to suppose that Napoleon would long maintain the stipulations of the treaties of Paris; the indignation excited throughout the country by these treaties had been one of the causes of the expulsion of the Bourbons. Would he have dared to regard them as an eternal engagement? The nation, above all the army, whose strength placed on a war footing had roused ambition, would they not have impelled the Chief of State to seize the first occasion to recover, at least, the line of the Rhine and the Alps?

In weighing these divers considerations we can easily conceive the doable perplexity in which his return had plunged the coalesced powers, and the resolutions that were the natural consequences of it. The conviction that the army alone had caused this revolution, and the fear of seeing the thrones at the mercy of military chieftains, joined to a desire of consolidating the shares of the conquests made from the empire; such were certainly the true incentives of the monarchs; either was sufficiently powerful to determine them; but it appeared very difficult to decide, whether the danger of substituting for Napoleon a government feeble in itself, and imposed upon them, was not greater than the ill effects of his return in assuring new revolutions.

The external embarrassments resulting from the acts of the Congress of Vienna, were not the only ones felt by Napoleon, because the Duke d'Angoulême being at Bordeaux at the time of his landing, had taken immediate measures for disputing the empire with him. Louis XVIII. had ordered this prince to establish at Toulouse the seat of a royal government, and had appointed him his Lieutenant in the south of France. From Toulouse, where he had rapidly organized resistance in concert with M. de Vitrolles and the Count de Damas, the Duke had repaired to Marseilles, where he had met with similar ovations on the part of this parasitical population, whose first wishes are mercantile wealth and substantial interest. Through the aid of a few regiments that remained faithful, and especially of the fanatical inhabitants of Languedoc, where religious dissensions were blended with the political quarrels, the Duke organized three columns with which he ascended the Rhone to retake Lyons and Grenoble; but defection also began in this body; two regiments declared for Napoleon, and the 10th of the line alone preserved a thousand soldiers for the prince, who here joined from six to seven thousands national guards.

After having beaten General Debelle at Loriol on the Drôme, he advanced on Valence; but the imperial officers sent to Toulouse and Montpelier, had succeeded in having the tri-coloured flag displayed in these two cities, and their garrisons, to declare for the Emperor. Meanwhile, Dauphiny also pronounced against the Bourbons, and Grouchy, ordered to Lyons, was preparing the means for smothering this feeble spark of civil war, by sending many small columns on Valence. The prince, closely pressed by General Gilley, and learning that the departments in his rear had recognized the imperial government, signed on the 9th April, at Pont-Saint-Esprit, a convention by which he consented to evacuate France and embark. Grouchy, in obedience to his orders, refused at first to ratify this act, which Napoleon however hastened to sanction.

Meanwhile, vexatious troubles breaking out in la Vendée, had forced fifteen thousand veterans to be detached thither under General Lamarque; this officer, previously distinguished for his activity, together with that of General Fravot, had suppressed the fire of civil war, the more formidable in this section of the country than in the rest of France, as much because of its locality as of the obstinate and devoted character of the inhabitants. Notwithstanding, however, the death of Larochejacquelin, killed in the Battle of Mathes, and the successes obtained at Saint-Giles and Roche-Servières, hostilities did not actually cease till after the Battle of Waterloo.

"While these things were happening in France, and at the Congress of Vienna, Murat still chanced to complicate his brother-in-law's position, by rising in arms in a way well worthy his eccentric and adventurous character. Informed of the negotiations that had taken place between France and Austria to depose him, he demanded of the latter a passage into Italy to reap vengeance for the threats of the ministry of Louis XVIII: he might have well known that this would be refused him. At the news of Napoleon's landing, Murat at once hoped to make amends for his defection in 1814. He was persuaded that the time had arrived for him to play a grand part, and that in promising the people of Italy a national insurrection, he might yet render himself the arbiter of great events.

On the 22nd of March, he debouched from Ancona with forty thousand men, drove the Austrians from Césène, and favoured by the population of Bologna and Modena, rapidly invaded the states situated on the Po, up to the gates of Placentia, while another column invaded the Roman states and Tuscany. He everywhere circulated proclamations, announcing that his object was to reunite the Italians under one banner, and in its name to take possession of the provinces he traversed: he even meditated the invasion of Lombardy through Piedmont, when his progress was arrested by the declarations of the English minister who menaced him with war.

The Austrians soon reassembled and hurled against him General Bianchi, with twenty-five or thirty thousand men. Leaving Florence with a majority of his forces, this general marched by Foligno, so as to cut off Murat's retreat, while Neipperg threatened him by the route of Ancona. The king of Naples was obliged to retire precipitately to avoid this untoward result; the decisive *rencontre* took place at Tolentino, on the 2nd of May; the Neapolitans, completely routed, dispersed in all directions. Murat, who has regained his capital with a slender escort, abandoned even by his warmest partisans, is constrained to fly from Naples and seek refuge in France; he lands at Toulon. A compact signed at Capua, by his Lieutenants, on the 20th of May, leads back Ferdinand IV. to the throne of the two Sicilies.

Nothing was ever more ill-timed than this affray. If Austria had had the least inclination to retrace her steps regarding the declarations of the 13th of March, this rendered it impossible; and in even supposing that the cabinet of Vienna was resolved to persist, everything should be avoided that tended to bind closer the ties of the coalition. In a military point of view, this was taking the initiative much too soon, because hostilities were commenced even before Napoleon's *entrée* into Paris was known, so that he was far from being able to second him. As a diversion, the king of Naples could do much, but the desire to act a principal part in the war was an absurdity.[14]

Thus, on two occasions did Murat compromise the Empire, the first by declaring for its enemies; the second in arming himself mal a propos. He expiated by a chivalric death, the two faults that had precipitated him from his throne; as a soldier, his will be a glorious memory.

Meanwhile, the sad result of this strange attempt, the success of the Austrians, and the advices that reached France of what was happening at Vienna, and in all the rest of Europe, was of a nature to inspire just fears in the least prejudiced minds. A formidable war threatened anew the national existence, and all hope of diverting the storm by concessions had vanished; Napoleon had to decide either to brave it, or to shun it most cowardly: between two such resolutions could a man of his character hesitate? If his personal honour had alone been at stake, he had had the power to sacrifice it to the future of France; but was not the honour of the nation more involved even than his own? A population of thirty millions, who had just elevated the greatest citizen to the throne, could not, because of a diplomatic declaration emanating from a foreign congress, drive away this adopted chief, and submit to the yoke they wished to impose!

Some mighty voices have however been raised, reproaching Napoleon for having continued on the throne after the reception of these declarations from Vienna. According to their views, he should have frankly exposed to the French people the position he held in the eyes of Europe, now alarmed and in arms against him, then have proposed to the nation the three following propositions for its decision:

1st. To place itself without delay at the mercy of Louis XVIII.

---

14. Many persons think that Murat was prompted by Napoleon to invade Italy, thus facilitating his enterprise by giving occupation to the Austrians. This had been well after he saw the impossibility of maintaining peace; but if he nourished a hope, this was most imprudent, and in either case the time was very ill chosen. It is then more than probable, that he was exceedingly annoyed by it.

2nd. To proclaim on the contrary Napoleon II., with a regency, or any other government that seemed preferable.

3rd or lastly. To declare the nullity of the abdication at Fontainbleau, in again awarding the Empire to Napoleon himself.

If the nation had adopted this last, then the fate of France had been irrevocably bound to his own, and any abandonment had been cowardice and felony.

The fervent and thoughtless apostles of national sovereignty might find something specious in these ideas, but at bottom they were devoid of all wisdom. In the first place, Napoleon did not immediately despair of leading Austria, and perhaps Russia, to more favourable views of his cause; he renewed his attempts, and even sent General Flahaut to Vienna with this intention. Subsequently, he had too much pride to submit thus to a sort of proscription that would have wounded a prince least capable of reigning, and which must have seemed doubly humiliating to a captain as illustrious as himself. Finally, it is probable that he still loved power too much, to follow the example of Charles V. and Victor Armédée, and seek repose in a cloister. Besides, could he entertain the idea of flying from France as proscribed, where Louis XVIII. had not failed to return, accompanied by a portion of the coalition? Would this not be delivering all those who were devoted to his cause, to the fury of a reaction?

Moreover, in abdicating early in April, to whom would he have intrusted his power, there being then no constituted authority? A beautiful conception truly, that of leaving France for three months without a government, at a time when eight hundred thousand men were bursting in upon her! There was no choice in the case; he had to fly while supplicating Louis XVIII. to re-enter his capital, or he had to fight. The alternative was a painful one, the chances were frightful, but alas! he had none other: and if well seconded, Napoleon felt the deep conviction of triumphing over his enemies.

Other Aristarchus', as reckless as those were timid, have pretended that far from yielding to the storm, the Emperor should have anticipated it, and at once availing himself of the first enthusiasm of the people, had shown to what extent he was yet formidable, by invading Belgium, and proclaiming liberty throughout Europe; whereas his pacific attitude lulled the nation into fancied security. Pitiable declamation! A people in blouses, and armed with pikes, cannot be hurled against the warlike legions of entire Europe. A grand army was necessary, and to obtain one, it was all important sacredly to preserve the nucleus that existed, to be increased by means of this very population that was being levied and organized. To this end, nothing had been effected, and the pacific attitude charged to Napoleon, consisted in sixteen hours daily labour for three months, to create this army. He increased the regiments of the line from two to five battalions, and reinforced those of cavalry with two squadrons; he ordered the organizing of 200 battalions of national *gardes mobiles*, 40 battalions of the old and new guard, and 20 regiments of marines. The old disbanded soldiers were all recalled to their standards, the conscriptions of 1814 and 1815 were levied; even the retired officers and soldiers were induced to join. By the 1st of June, that is, in two months, the effective strength of the French army had been augmented from 200,000 to 414,000: by the month of September, he could have counted on 700,000 men, but time failed him.

It would be absurd to believe that in the midst of these preparations Napoleon had not thought of the invasion of Belgium, to secure the defensive line of the Rhine. From the day after his arrival at Paris, this question had been debated, but more than one obstacle had to be surmounted.

At first, there were in hand but 40,000 men, la Vendée had revolted, the Duke of Angoulême was marching on Lyons, and the Marseillese on Grenoble. It behoved him to be master at home before wishing to be master abroad. A still stronger reason hindered this invasion. How was such a step to be reconciled to the letter, in which the Emperor offered the sovereigns a sincere and durable peace? If he had been rash in calculating on the friendliness of all, there were still some motives for relying on the good-will of his father-in-law. The Emperor of Austria had sought to prevent his dethronement in 1814; at the time of his return, the discussion with Russia grew warm respecting the division of Gallicia, and the fate of Saxony.

There was every reason to hope that the cabinet of Vienna would consent in 1815, to what its negotiator had himself proposed in 1814: to uphold the Emperor on the throne, if he consented to abandon Italy. Napoleon made this proposition, and notwithstanding the famous declaration of the 13th March, they still hoped to see the father of Maria Louisa return to his first views. Nevertheless, the French have censured Napoleon with an inclination for war; public opinion having declared for peace, repelled all idea of aggression, before knowing whether the maintenance of this peace was possible.

Even admitting that it was easy to foresee the issue of these pacific measures, little could be gained by hastening to Brussels, yet guarded by an army of occupation of the Germanic Confederation: Luxemburg and Mentz no longer belonged to France, and these places, as well as Holland, giving the allies many *débouchés* on the left of the Rhine, it is not certain that any benefit had accrued from this invasion; the fighting would have commenced on the Meuse and Moselle, instead of on the Sambre, that is all. Taking the least probable supposition, their succeeding in subjecting Antwerp and Luxemburg without a siege, it would be necessary to throw into them strong garrisons, and the French were not at all in condition to do so. If, on the contrary, these important places continued in the power of the enemy, of what use was Brussels, surrounded by Maestricht, Luxemburg, Bergen-on-Zoom, and Antwerp? Was it not wiser to hold the skeletons of the old regiments in hand, in order to double the number of effectives by a new organization, than to scatter them through Belgium?

It has been said that it would have been necessary for him to commence anew a complete revolution, taking advantage of all the arbitrary resources it creates, and to rouse all the passions, profiting by their blind devotion, as without it France could not be saved. This was Fouché's advice, and especially Carnot's, who remained a thorough Jacobin under the cloak of Count. Many causes prevented Napoleon from having recourse to these means; the first was that he dreaded popular commotions, and with reason too, as he had no rein by which to guide them, and they consume those by whom excited; the second was that he was not at all convinced that anarchy and the overthrow of all social order were infallible means of saving a nation: these succeeded in 1793, through a concurrence of unexampled circumstances, that will probably never again recur.

Besides, whatever fear the Emperor had of these popular storms, he believed it necessary to excite the masses to a certain degree, not however without fixing it within certain limits; the task is difficult and the path a slippery one. To unchain the revolutionary tiger with a deliberate purpose, comes within the province only of such madmen as Marat and Robespierre, or of extravagant men devoid of all experience. After having authorized federated societies, destined to rouse the public mind for the defence of the country, he was active in preventing them from extending their action to affect the social order; to accomplish this, a suitable strength in the administration, and forecast in the institutions, were requisite; but it was very difficult to sustain this double-faced performance.

Because of the new elections, Napoleon was actually to find himself in presence of republicans conquered the 18th *Brumaire*, of royalists who did not desire his empire, and of anarchists who wanted no government at all. But by flattering the hopes of the first two, and the follies of the last, he counted on their influence and patriotic declamations to excite the people to arms. While setting at work these revolutionary elements, the chief of State hoped to direct the employment of a power sufficiently firm to repress anarchy. Unfortunately, those over-excited soon perceived that the reign of clubs had passed forever, and held forth his caution as a proof of his thirst for power, while they constituted the sole guaranty for social order and for those who were to guide the vessel of State amidst the frightful tempests by which it was threatened.

The assembly of the *Champ de Mai* was at hand; it was necessary at once, to explain frankly the changes that should be made in the institutions of the empire. Napoleon had announced his intention of concerting these changes with the deputies of the nation which would be delegated for this purpose; but the declarations of the Congress of Vienna, and the preparations of the new coalition leaving little doubt of an impending war, he had to choose between the necessity of sending the electors back to their homes, so as to seize an indefinite dictatorial power, or to present, himself, the modifications which he was disposed to make in the exercise of this power, knowing that it would be imprudent to depart for the army, leaving France without a legal government, a prey to dogmatical disputes, and to the shocks of factions.

It is probable, however, that Napoleon was not sorry in having this plausible pretext for consolidating his power; because, if dogmatical discussions on constitutions are always stormy in an assembly of four or five hundred persons, and usually result in the triumph of doctrines the least calculated for securing the necessary strength and stability to the government, how could such a discussion be carried on, even through delegates, in the presence of a hundred thousand electors?

The emperor judged it, then, indispensable to take the initiative, in the modifications necessary for blending harmoniously the ancient institutions of the empire, with the liberal opinions with which they had clashed. These modifications were discussed in a council composed of ministers and the council of state, to which was invited Benjamin Constant, the most influential of those theoretical publicists, who were so noisy in the tribune and such poor actors when governing.

Desirous of gaining over the ex-tribune, who was constantly at the head of all the *doctrinaires* opposition, Napoleon had him called the 14th April, for particular consultation on these important measures, before submitting them to the council. He exposed his views with a *frankness*, a *coolness*, and an impartiality, for which Benjamin Constant had the kindness seriously to reproach him after his fall; as if such questions should ever be treated with passion, impulse or dissimulation. His letters on the hundred days in which he gives an account of this interview, are not the least curious among the writings published by Napoleon's adversaries for their own justification!

"The nation," said he to him, "has reposed free from all political agitation for twelve years; the past year she has been without war; this double repose has rendered her in need of activity. *She wishes or believes she wishes a public tribune and assemblies: she has not always wanted them,* she cast herself at my feet when I reached the capital. You, who attempted an opposition, should remember it: where was your support, your strength? Nowhere. I have taken less authority than I have been invited to assume.

"Now, everything is changed; the taste for constitutions, debates and harangues appear to have returned. Nevertheless, be not deceived, it is but the minority who wish it. The people only want me: have you not seen them, pressing upon my steps, precipitating themselves from the mountains, seeking me, saluting me But a signal from me is necessary, for them to fall upon the royalists and nobles..... But I do not wish to be the king of a Jacquerie.... If there be a means of governing with a constitution, at the proper time I demand nothing better, though this be not so easy as it is thought I have desired the empire of the world, and to secure it unlimited power was necessary; solely to govern France, a constitution may do better

"Although this is still a problem, it can be tried. I have wished the empire of the world: who, in my place, had not wished it? The world invited me to govern it people and governors, in emulation of each other, cast themselves under my sceptre... Let me then. see the system that will seem to you possible; give me your thoughts. Public discussions, free elections, responsible

---

15. Napoleon might have told the truth when he expressed this idea; but he was soon convinced that he had erred, or at least that he intended this liberty with all the means for repressing license.

ministers, liberty of the press I am willing for all this; I am convinced on this subject.[15]

"I am the man of the people: if they really wish liberty, I owe it to them I have never dreamed of oppressing them to please myself I had grand designs, fate has decided upon them. I am no longer a conqueror, I can no longer be one I have but one mission, that of lifting up France and giving her a suitable government. I am not willing to raise false hopes. I permit it to be said that negotiations are pending, there are none. I foresee a difficult struggle, a protracted war; though I desire peace I will be unable to obtain it but by force of victories; the nation must support me. In exchange she will want liberty: she has as much of it as it is possible to give her without falling into anarchy. The situation is a new one; I demand but to be enlightened. I am growing old; the repose of a constitutional king might suit me; it will suit my son still better."

We perceive from these words, that Napoleon felt the delicacy of the task imposed on him. Those, inimical to all power, who have accused him of duplicity during this short reign of a hundred days, because he did not wish a return of the *régime* of 1793 or 1799, can rest assured on the very assertions of Benj. Constant, that he frankly adopted the deliberative assemblies and the public tribune, as a necessity of the epoch, while far from partaking of the universal infatuation on the subject. Nevertheless, they suspect and accuse him, as they did Louis XVIII., of insincerity in this species of political conversion. If the principles that were in full force at the establishment of the empire, proved that experience in affairs had very much modified the liberal ideas he had professed during the first years of the revolution, everything bears us out in the belief that he would have respected the new institutions promised, had the other established powers sincerely desired to remain within their limits, and been well satisfied that their true constitutional mission is to second the government and not to restrain or annul its action.

We have already stated, that Napoleon did not fail to recognize the advantages that might be expected from assemblies; but he also appreciated the immense dangers they present, when prudent and strong institutions do not sufficiently regulate their influence and procedure: he thought that modern charters and the political education of the French had not as yet reached this point. Experience will prove if he was wrong: meanwhile, I will be permitted to present some observations drawn from more recent events, and which, on the contrary, bear us out in believing that he was perfectly right.

The dogmas on liberty that have created so much sensation in our day, and which he, with many others, had professed in good faith, are certainly of the most alluring nature if applied to man individually; but when applied collectively, to societies called nations, and to governmental ideas, we acknowledge that this term is often greatly abused. The result is a sort of confusion in constitutional language, an obscure metaphysics that have produced the strangest political creeds.

Men of weight and learning have laid down as a principle, that authority, that is to say government, being an encroacher by nature, finds itself as a consequence the natural enemy of liberty. With such a beautiful system as a starting point, it is very plain that all men calling themselves friends of liberty, must be regarded as born enemies to authority, whether it emanates from a consul, a prefect, an emperor, or a king. Thus has it resulted that administrations, whether public, royal, imperial, or otherwise, established for the protection of public interests and private rights; functionaries who should administer justice, protect the lives and property of the citizens, organize fleets and armies, promote and regulate public instruction, conduct wars, deliberate upon and conclude alliances, negotiate treaties, dig canals, construct for- tresses, prepare and develop the national strength: these authorities in a word, who should be the pride of every well-organized nation, have been transformed by these strange doctrines into public enemies . . . . . in to objects of suspicion and hate.

Let me not be accused of exaggeration: I appeal to all those who have occupied a position of any eminence in France; there is not one of them who does not today include a good portion of those he governed, among the number of his adversaries or detractors. It is necessary to state that the apostles of these singular maxims, have not always been hair-brained youths just from college, or proletarians without name, and without existence. The most ardent have been found among the writers who have acquired celebrity or popularity; among grave magistrates; in the highest grades of the army; finally, among the legislators who have re-echoed them from the tribune, amid the acclamations of all the adepts; so that a good number of deputies, led by these utopianists, were persuaded that the chambers also were in duty bound to enchain and obstruct authority, whenever an occasion offered.

With such ideas a nation becomes ungovernable and rushes to

inevitable ruin, unless a violent catastrophe, or a great man gives renewed vigour to social order by placing it on surer bases; the bloody lessons of experience are the sole remedies for an evil so deeply rooted. Struck with these inconveniences, Napoleon was convinced that to govern well with such elements, there was no institution that could give too much strength to the public administration, and it should be acknowledged to his glory that all he did in a contrary sense was forced upon him by circumstances.

It should also be acknowledged that he always rendered justice to those estimable men, free from all feeling of personal ambition, who in good faith professed these exaggerated doctrines of liberty, such as Lanjuinais, Benj. Constant, Lafayette, &c., &c. As private individuals, or as philosophers, civic crowns perhaps should be awarded them; but as politicians and founders of fundamental institutions, they were in his eyes, but apostles of crude theories, more fatal than useful; because, by substituting unceasingly declamations and phrases in place of true genius and the art of governing, they will always put a nation at the mercy of the most rash and most crafty rhetorician, and lead to eternal conflicts between the executive power and those by whom it is so much coveted.

Undoubtedly, what is called public liberty,—constitutional government,—equilibrium of the three powers are very beautiful things, seductive theories, perhaps very good with the counterpoise of a powerful aristocracy.[16] I think, too, that they might agree with absolute democracy in a new and isolated nation like the United States of America, in the midst of a vast continent, with no neighbours but settlements of savages without power, or without ambition, because in such a case internal commotions would be devoid of danger to the political powers of the country; but with a nation surrounded by formidable and jealous neighbours, with a nation whose old social body is composed of ancient feudal nobility, young war-like nobility, proud and turbulent *tiers état* and inflammable minds, it is altogether otherwise, or it would at least be necessary to rest the institutions on more solid bases than our modern charters have done.

So far, we will be permitted to believe with Napoleon, that posi-

---

16. If by public liberty, we understand individual liberty, equality in the eye of the law, and the concurrence of the nation, to a rational extent, in the framing of laws, nothing undoubtedly is more desirable. Even the liberty of the press confined within just bounds, may also be added. Everything beyond this, leads to license and anarchy.

tively the institution of three powers in *equilibrio*, has been but a beautiful fiction, the application of which does not correspond with the seductive theory. To be as admirable as it is thought, this political trinity should have that unity of faith and action belonging to the religious trinity; for say and do what we may, the *action* of a government should never be but *one* and *indivisible*. Whether it represents the nation among strangers, or dispenses justice at home, or organizes and disposes of the land and naval forces, which are the symbols of national power, its system and its progress should be uniform; there cannot be two in one state.

Now, if three independent powers, ever jealous of their influence and authority, are established, what means will you have of establishing this unity, indispensable in the direction of the grand affairs of the country? All assemblies in the world when adorned, right or wrong, with the title of representatives of the nation,[17] will be cavilling and usurping by their nature, especially if they have the initiative in the laws; because with this initiative they will be able to guide the vessel of state if they will, and they will wish it whenever they can. The evil would be without danger, if it were possible for an assembly, composed of small *specialitiés meeting now and then*, to be qualified of itself to rule a great nation; but as the impossibility of it is acknowledged, it forcibly results therefrom, that by according the initiative to this assembly, you give it all the means of perplexing the administration and rendering the same impossible, without giving it the means of governing.

Nothing could flow from such a state of things but endless uncertainty, an unheard-of distress in the direction of affairs, and the impossibility of the government's determining on a stable system of foreign policy, that which is always the most decisive for the maintenance of a country's greatness. To this impossibility should be added that of fixing on a good system of military organization, from nothing previously prepared, for the contingent events that menaced the most important future interests of the state.

This perpetual clashing of the government and the elective chambers, deprived of an aristocratic counterpoise, will be. not only difficult to avoid or modify,—a dreadful instability in the personnel of the ministry will also result as a consequence; an inconsistency not the less hurtful to a state than the most threatening invasion, in producing but

---

17. Elective chambers are far from being always the faithful representations of the interests and wishes of the country: they often represent but a small fraction, perhaps, the most selfish and the least national.

a phantasmagorical magistracy, to which might be applied the famous verse of Corneille:

> *Ces petits souverains qu'on fait pour une année,*
> *Voyant d'un temps si court leur puissance bornée,*
> *Des plus heureux desseins font avorter le fruit,*
> *De peur de le laisser à celui qui les suit:*
> *Comme ils ont peu de part an bien dont ils ordonnent,*
> *Dans le champ du public largement ils moissonnent,*
> *Assurés que chacun leur pardonne aisément,*
> *Espérant à son tour un pareil traitement.*—Cinna.

In fact, what country could prosper, at home or abroad, with, apprenticed ministers, succeeding each other every six months, arid who are superseded before concluding their novitiate?

A man may be endowed with brilliant genius, and still require time in which to learn the duties of his department, and reflect on systems that might ameliorate its progress; and in foreign policy especially, what confidence can be inspired in her neighbours,—her natural allies,—by such instability? It were better if each minister were allowed a permanent under-secretary of state, who would at least preserve the tradition of all that would be beneficial and useful to the department; but far from recurring to these wise means, these innovators have laboured to abolish a portion of those that existed. Such a state of things, deplorable under an able king, would become mortal under a feeble prince or during a minority.

It will be said that the enmity of one of the three powers could be counterbalanced by the united will of the other two. This would be true, if we entertained at least the thought of establishing, in the fundamental law, that the union of two of these powers, twice ascertained, and in two different sessions, would suffice to sanction a law or any act whatever? notwithstanding the opposition of the third; but it has never been done; and this may perchance be unwise, because, since you desire an equilibrium between three authorities, it would be well to admit that two of them represent the majority, and that it is absurd to desire that one alone have the power of annihilating the wishes of the other two: in such a case, the minority makes the law.

It will be answered that the charter might provide for this, in giving royalty the right of dissolution, and that of nominating new peers, and giving the chambers the right of rejecting proposed laws and refusing taxation. These means are at once violent and inefficacious remedies, because, in order that the dissolution of the chambers be of any service, it would be necessary to admit that all the electors were consummate politicians, and capable of deciding on the differences that had caused it. But such electors will never exist. In fact, if it be true that this measure is often the result of miserable personal intrigues and of a deplorable party spirit, on the merits of which an elector would be much perplexed to pass any judgement whatever, how can a favourable result be expected? How would a new election condemn an intrigue, the plot of which had been contrived by the very men who declare themselves the directors of public opinion?

Let us even take things like true optimists, and suppose, as these things should be, that the dissolution was only the result of a serious struggle between two systems of politics strongly opposed to each other, and not that of ambitious individuals. In this case, is it not evident that the electors would be unable to decide which of the two systems would best suit the country? Questions present themselves, not only in internal politics, but still more in foreign policy, which, though enveloped in appearances the most seductive, contain elements of life and death to the power of a state. Will these questions be wisely settled by the licensed dealers and small land-holders, when the greatest intellects of the nation are perplexed and divided as to the system to be followed?

And then, is it not known how electors choose their local deputies, who perhaps represent very well their *arrondissements*, but often ill-understand the general interests of France? Is it not known, what part intrigue and *camaraderie* play in this choice? Are we ignorant of the influence exercised by the journals at the capital, and of the spirit in which they are edited; what their candour, their impartiality, their wisdom, the profundity of their views, their pretended patriotism? With such elements, what can be the result of a dissolution? Will they dare say that the re-election will present the real wishes of France, when twenty or thirty votes, perhaps the most indifferent in the country, exacted through intrigue and party spirit, will have been acquired by the opposition and secured its triumph?

Is it not frightful to think, that by the aid of a factitious majority, certain ambitious men, without prudence or depth of thought, will be able to secure the adoption of a principle anarchical in its character and destructive of all national greatness; a principle which would not only disturb the state internally, but would remove the means of waging war at once useful and of a result almost certain, to be followed by foolish and desperate struggles, to sustain Utopian ideas and flatter popular passions? A singular equilibrium this, that will give to twenty deputies the power of annulling a good system, adopted by the king, the ministers, the chamber of peers, the council of state, and even half of the elective chamber, less these twenty votes! And such institutions will be called the perfectibility of the human mind, the *chef-d'oeuvre* of a progressive age!!

The appointment of the new peers, conceded to royalty, has not, perhaps, the same inconveniences as the dissolution, but it has some others. When made in small numbers, the spirit of the chamber may not be changed; made inconsiderately, and in larger numbers, it debases this precious institution, the sole barrier against levelling demagoguism. A wise government should not have recourse to such measures merely to maintain a ministry, but only when the vessel of state is in imminent danger.

We thus see that the Trinitarian system actually offers more chances of rupture, than of efficacious means for securing a useful and advantageous equilibrium; since royalty, in striking the elective chambers, strikes falsely, and nothing usually remains but wounds.

The means possessed by the elective chambers for opposing a project or a system approved by royalty and the peers, are still worse, because the refusal of any particular law would be insignificant if it was not at times a question of existence; the refusal of the budget alone, could overthrow the ministry. This presents the gravest of constitutional questions. To what extent would an assembly actually in a minority in the Trinitarian government, have the right to disorganize the state throughout, by refusing to levy the necessary taxes for settling the accounts of the army and navy, and securing the payment of magistrates and the public debt? And this, perhaps, to gratify a miserable party rancour, a rancour actually arising from the fact, that the monarch or the ministry enjoy a transcendent capacity of which the proud mediocrity are jealous.[18] No, such a charter is not perfection; as it gives all power for evil without giving an equal measure of power for good.

I do not pretend to deduce from this that all constitutional charters

---

18. If a refusal of the budget was voted by a majority of twenty votes, the consequence would be, that twenty deputies would have had a power superior to that of the king, peers, ministers, and two hundred deputies who voted with the government. These twenty men would proclaim themselves the voice of France, and would, through self-love or ambition, disorganize the country.

are deceptions, and that all governments with chambers are impossible; I only wish to say, that the combinations adopted up to this time have not fulfilled the object for which they were intended, and that to be successful, recourse to other methods is necessary.

The proposition is a simple one; for a representative government to be a good one, and able to proceed successfully, the constitution must be a good one: when the institutions are perverted, the representative government is the most deplorable of all. Now, to base a constitutional monarchy on proper foundations and to frame a good charter, it is necessary, above all things, firmly to establish the fundamental truths upon which it should rest, namely:

1st. That the popular masses are, by their nature, called upon to be governed, not to govern; that it is the province of the middle classes to represent the democratic interests of the country, and to discharge the duties appertaining thereto in a just and equitable manner.

2nd. That the chamber of peers should represent the national *notabilités* of all kinds that exist, and the interests connected with them.

3rd. That the executive power, that is, the throne, represents the nation and all its interests among foreign powers; it also represents the interests of all classes of citizens among each other, since it is by nature, as it is its duty to conciliate the interests of all, not desiring the good of one to the detriment of others, except in a very few cases where the general interest of the country imperiously demands this exception.

4th. That the democratic elective chamber, not representing the entire nation, but only a portion of the middle classes, will be powerless in any case to arrogate to itself the sovereignty, without committing a signal and criminal usurpation.

These are grand and incontestable truths,—though sad prejudices, bad passions, and sometimes bad governments, appear at times to have given them the lie.

When perfectly convinced of these truths, which will not be the less real for having remained unacknowledged by the present generation, then you may perhaps be able to establish good institutions; but as long as you proclaim popular sovereignty, the sovereignty of an elective chamber; as long as you boldly profess dogmas tending to treat as an enemy this executive power, designed to conciliate, defend, and unite into one, these interests of your different classes and different localities; finally, as long as your laws and your discourses tend to debase and annul this power which is the true guaranty of national greatness, then you may attempt a thousand theories, establish a thousand charters: they will always prove to be works of deception, without consistency, and fatal to the country.

If a purely democratic elective chamber without an aristocratic counterpoise, and in session only during certain months of the year, wishes to rule the state, anarchy is inevitable; because, in order that the wheels of government possess the necessary action, it is indispensable that the elective chamber be an instrument and not an obstacle. In a word, it is necessary in a monarchy that the king be king and the deputies be his best counsellors. . . . If you insist on being governed by chambers, *or by one chamber*, then have a senate for life, which is recruited through its own proper choice, and not by department elections,—an aristocratic senate, like that of Rome and Berne; otherwise, every act will be of short duration, and the state becoming the prey of intrigue, will be consumed or fall into endless revolutions.

We can conclude from the preceding:—

1st. That if the equilibrium of the constitutional powers is the most important and most desirable end to which a fundamental charter can aspire, this equilibrium must be real and perfectly poised, or the entire governmental edifice will be found falsified and compromised.

2nd. That it is dangerous to accord the initiative of the laws to the chambers, it being sufficient to give them the right of demanding from the ministry, a law on a determined object that these may have lost sight of.

3rd. That the *pure* and *simple* dissolution of the elective chambers is a work of deception, of which intrigue will generally gather all the fruits, if an appeal can be had to the electors themselves, or if the law does not interdict the re-election of the same deputies; because, to make a true appeal to the French nation, it would be necessary to appoint beforehand a certain number of extra deputies, or require the election of an entirely new deputation, to ascertain the opinion of the electoral body on the system that may have led to the dissolution.[19]

4th. That the usual budget should be voted at least for three or four years, and that extraordinary expenses or additional taxes should alone be voted annually.

---

19. The extra deputies could be appointed beforehand, so that in case of a dissolution, there would be a new vote more generally authenticated. This is merely indicating a defect in the equilibrium of the powers, without pretending to state the means of correcting it.

5th. Lastly, that it would be necessary to find means for preventing party intrigues from paralyzing two of the powers, and a large portion of the third, otherwise, the equilibrium of the powers and the government of the majority will be a double illusion.

Without these precautions, the governing of a great nation through elective assemblies, *meeting temporarily, and composed of purely democratic elements*, will be as painful a task as that of rolling the rock of Sisyphus. If examples from the Romans be cited in opposition, I will answer those who understand the institutions of this great people so superficially, that their government was not an elective democracy, and that the aristocratic senate appointed for life, or hereditary patricians, are the only assemblies that have ever properly directed the policy of a country; again, those which history recalls, were always forced to recognize the supremacy of an executive power, either under the name of consul or under the title of Doge and the council of ten, whose powers were anything but liberal. Not that I prefer aristocratic or patrician republics, they are the most exclusive and most tyrannical governments. I have already given my views in a previous volume,- where I have proved *that hereditary monarchy, tempered by wise laws, and not a debased and impotent monarchy*, was the most rational form for a great civilized nation.

I perceive that I am led away by my theme, and that it is time to return to Napoleon, whose views rather than mine own must be explained. Whatever might be his maxims on the inconveniences of assemblies, the circumstances under which he found himself were still of a nature to double his fears, and the following passage that we borrow from one of his addresses, leaves no doubt as to his views on this subject:

> In time of war, if you succeed in electrifying deliberative assemblies, they may become centres of enthusiasm and of devotion to the country, but they have also more than one dangerous aspect. If a division takes place between them and the executive power, then the government is impossible, there is no longer strength in the conduct of affairs; victory is necessary to them at any cost; because, at the least reverse, terror takes possession of the timid and moderate, who ordinarily constitute the greatest number; we do not always find assemblies as furious as the convention, placed by the regicide between victory and the scaffold, and forced to conquer or display a frightful energy.

These examples are exceptions.

Under ordinary circumstances, and especially in assemblies of peaceable proprietors, the least reverse strikes the timid with fear of perils, and awakens all pretensions in the breast of the ambitious. Those eager for celebrity, popularity and domination, set themselves up from their proper sphere into counsellors to the prince; they pretend to know and decide all things; if their advice is rejected, from counsellors they become factious; then, finally, after having undermined all the elements of confidence and power, they preach a revolt in the name of a public good of their own fashioning, the source of which is entirely in their imaginations. Then the prince must submit to their yoke or break it; and in either case, he is obliged to peril the government and the state, at a moment when he should triple his force to resist the foreigner.

Napoleon performed, then, a great act of self-denial, in deciding to proclaim the establishment of two chambers, with public tribunes; still he preferred this course to the chance of a single constituent assembly, that had raised controversies in the presence of formidable enemies, and whose powers being almost unlimited, had entirely annulled his own. Moreover, by reserving to himself the initiative of the laws, after the example of Louis XVIII., he calculated on confining their action within just bounds. Such was the dominant idea while drawing up the additional act.

Benjamin Constant was charged with draughting the imperial thoughts, modified by some of his own; this work, submitted to the council composed of the ministers and the council of state, did not fail to find censors; the majority of the members would have preferred an entirely new constitution, deliberated upon by a national assembly, not only because formally announced in the decrees of Lyons, but it being important not to expose it to the same reflections that had destroyed the granted charter. Fouché himself raised many other objections to the debated project. This political Proteus, ever ready to embrace the opinion he judged to be in the ascendant, wished to give the chambers the initiative of the laws, and to make Napoleon a *veto king like that of* 1791.[20]

---

20. We are aware that the populace gave no other name to Louis XVI. than *Monsieur Veto*, because he was only invested with the power of opposing everything, while the first attribute of the administration that knows the wants of the country, is to prepare and contrive everything and submit the same to the chambers. This was reversing the governmental edifice.

He also wished the different statutes of the empire, that would remain in the new fundamental law, to be discussed by the chambers, and disposed of according to their good pleasure. Lastly, he demanded a new assembly of the *Champ de Mai* for the following year, that the same deputies might return to discuss the proposed compact, and again surrender everything in question.

From the principles I have frequently exposed, it was difficult for the objections of the members of the council to shake the emperor's convictions; on the contrary, he depicted his fears so eloquently, that he succeeded in persuading them that the supreme law of threatened public safety, and the possibility of modifying the institutions at a later period, with the legal concurrence of the two chambers, militated strongly in favour of his project.

He consequently proclaimed, on the 22nd April, an additional act to the constitutions of the empire. This act established a chamber of hereditary peers, a chamber of elective deputies of six hundred and twenty-nine members; granted a special deputation to commerce and industry; proclaimed the liberty of the press, the responsibility of ministers, the independence and irremovability of judges, trial by jury, even for offences by the press, and personal and religious liberty.[21]

However, to relieve this act from the semblance of illegality that might be alleged against it, it should have been sent to the departments, as well as to the army and navy, for the sanction of a national vote, the result of which would be proclaimed to the assembly of the *Champ de Mai*, whose meeting was adjourned for this purpose, to the 1st June.

Such institutions were certainly more than sufficient for governing a nation the most sensitive on the subject of its liberties, especially after the decree of Lyons abolishing the feudal and privileged nobility. And, in fact, liberty was so enlarged, that Châteaubriand, with a correctness of judgment that was not always his most characteristic trait, thus wrote to Louis XVIII.:

> Napoleon is caught in his own net; the additional act will be fatal to him; if observed, there is in the main sufficient liberty to overthrow the usurper.

---

21. Each *arrondissement* had a deputy direct, but in addition, the departments had also their deputies; so that there were 238 deputies of departments, 368 of *arrondissements*, and 23 of manufactures and commerce. In 1830, the department deputies were suppressed, leaving but those of the *arrondissements*, and this is the greatest error that has been committed.

And Benjamin Constant himself boasted of this decision, to prove the excellence of the doctrines introduced by himself and friends! Singular eulogy to deliver on these doctrines, that of proving that they could destroy the political edifice, whose stability and solidity should have been their work!

However, though this compact was adopted by two millions of voters, it became the subject of all criticism—all parties judged it most unmercifully through the medium of their passions and interests. The incorrigible speculators of republican theories censured Napoleon for not having been satisfied with the consulate for life, and attributed to a miserable spirit of nepotism, the wise foresight which had decided him in re-establishing hereditary succession in the supreme magistracy, as being the only safeguard for the existence of great nations.

Other ideologists, less insane, however, than the republicans, wished to accord the initiative of the laws to the chambers, a dogma incompatible with the interests of the state, and with the regular functions of the wheels of government.

Demagogues wanted the *régime* of the forum or of popular societies. The royalists were dissatisfied with the abolition of feudal distinctions; the levellers, with their having preserved the titles given under the empire as a recompense for signal services, and more so with their having maintained a chamber of hereditary peers that wounded their pride or their foolish pretensions, and which Napoleon wished to uphold, precisely with the hope of leading, in time, to a non-feudal aristocracy, sufficiently powerful to serve as an equilibrium to royalty, on the one hand, and the multitude on the other.

Finally, a last class of opponents to the additional act, without blaming its source, presented it as a capital blunder, an act of deception the more deplorable, as it would offend all the electors of the nation and the deputies of the land and naval forces, convoked at Paris to effect, through their delegates, these very changes, in which Napoleon had singly taken the initiative. They pretended, moreover, that the time was not opportune for such a measure, when even the institutions promulgated were indispensable for preserving to the throne the strength that constituted its *éclat* as well as its guaranty, or giving the state that vigour, without which it could not attain its highest destiny. But none of these critics wished to take into consideration, the imperious circumstances under which France was to be thrown, by reason of the general league that menaced her, and this act, far from having been violent, was actually justified by the necessities of the times.

Fouché himself did not spare him his censure: covetous of power and influence, he was prompted on one side by what remained him of revolutionary doctrines, on the other by the desire of fixing bounds to the imperial power, either to render his own more necessary or prevent the emperor from ordering him into a species of exile, as in 1810, as soon as he could dispense with his services. At the news of the declaration of the 13th March, he judged, from all appearances, that the new throne was not the most stable, and with his habitual cunning, he in a measure intrigued at Vienna, to secure a reconciliation with the allies, and render himself useful to the government that would succeed Napoleon, should he be overcome.[22]

The services that this minister of police had rendered Metternich in 1809, facilitated the establishment of these clandestine connexions, of which he was too crafty to make a mystery, firmly convinced, moreover, of giving them the direction that would best answer his views. Now, these views consisted either in restraining the emperor's authority by means of powerful assemblies, influenced by himself and friends, or even in replacing his government by that of his son, the regency to be directed by himself; finally, as a last resource, he hoped to become the instrument and arbiter of a second restoration. Napoleon was on the eve of discovering these plots, when Fouché adroitly submitted to him the communications he had just received from the allies through the mediation of the Austrian minister, and the answer he thought of returning.

---

22. There are different versions of this subject. The memoirs of General Lamarque, and the *History of the Restoration*, by C———... have formally accused Fouché of having betrayed Napoleon.... Lucien Bonaparte seeks to justify him, at least as to his connexion with Austria. It seems certain that the declaration of the Congress of Vienna unsettled Fouché exceedingly, and that he conceived, from that time, that the emperor's power was unsteady; he judged, that he would either be forced to recur to the revolutionary propaganda of 1793, or would fall. Anxious to acquire sufficient influence on the future of France, to prevent the return of the Bourbons, or at least to render himself necessary to a second conditional restoration, he was no longer a devoted minister, and while rendering to Napoleon an account of his relations with Metternich, he could very well give them a clandestine turn that would eventually serve other ends.

The additional act displeased him the more as Napoleon took no notice of his objections: hence everything bears us out in the belief that he served him indifferently, and we are even assured that lie corresponded with Wellington before the battle of Waterloo. However, it is certain, that immediately after this battle, he assumed an attitude for throwing off Napoleon, if not by a crime, at least by a forced abdication, and even by an exile concerted with the allies.

Excited by the astonishing success of the new revolution that had just taken place, and by the preparations ordered for arming the nation, the sovereigns had no doubt purposely decided to separate the cause of Napoleon from that of France, so as to effect a division between the nation and his partisans, or even to obtain his voluntary retirement, by allowing him to conceive the possibility of placing his son on the throne with a regency. They consequently declared that they did not desire to interfere in the internal affairs of France, provided she procured another chief. They left to the nation the choice of a form of government, even a republic; but did not wish the emperor at any price. Either he had provoked these measures by his first overtures, or Metternich had himself taken the initiative. Fouché had not dared to conceal such an incident. He knew that to quiet Napoleon, it was easy for him to make an ostensible answer, so disposed by devious ways, as to be the means of entering into other combinations.

This ostensible answer, given the 8th May, could not be doubted: :

> In endeavouring to review all the expedients upon which the country could rest, Fouché sought to demonstrate that the maintenance of the emperor offered the greatest security to Europe. The restoration of Louis XVIII. would be an act of humiliation to France, and would never be upheld even with the aid of foreign bayonets. His being replaced by the younger branch of the family presented but little more stability, because the Duke d'Orleans would always have arrayed against him the royalists, republicans, and the party still more to be dreaded, the Bonapartists.[23]

> The prince offering a guaranty only to the doctrinaires of the revolution, would be forced to submit to their laws, which would insensibly lead to anarchy, confusion, and finally another revolution. The regency of Maria-Louisa with Napoleon II. would have the inconvenience of being influenced by Napoleon in the important foreign policy, without having those elements of internal strength which his single name would have secured against demagogues. The maintenance of his authority, tempered by constitutions that would prevent wars of ambition, and those gigantic levies of men that had rendered him so terrible to his neighbours, was then the sole means of securing to Europe the repose of which she stood so much in need.

---

23. It must not be forgotten that Fouché wrote this in 1815, Napoleon being not only alive but in power.

Moreover, Fouché was right, in pointing out the unusual manner of proclaiming the intention not to dictate laws to France, while imposing upon her the formal exclusion of the chief of her choice. He demonstrated that the independence of a great nation is one and indivisible, that it exists absolute and intact or does not exist at all; in a word, that it was no more a disgrace to have a government imposed than permitting a prohibition in the choice determined on.

In fact, the recent publication of the additional act, did no longer permit either France or Napoleon to return a different answer to the course of the cabinet at Vienna and of the allies; if this course had been taken at the place and time of the famous declaration of the 13th March, the emperor might have decided in favour of his son and of France, a sacrifice claimed by the sovereigns; it would have given it the appearance of a voluntary and spontaneous initiative in a generous action;[24] but after this solemn declaration, and after the additional act, nothing was left him but to reign and fight, or seek a coward's safety in flight. Convinced that the national honour was closely bound to his own, he redoubled his preparations to wage the war thrust upon him to the death, and all his efforts were exerted in exciting the same devotion and energy in the new authorities who were to share with him the burden of the government, and among the deputies of the *Champ de Mai,* convoked for the end of this month: perfectly persuaded that if he found this support, the legions of Europe would be crushed in their attacks upon France.

It must be acknowledged that the nation was too divided in opinion to permit Napoleon to rally it, entire; it was broken up into four portions of very different strengths:

1st. The partisans of fallen royalty, who were still numerous, and counted in their ranks the greater portion of the constitutional doctrinaires.

2nd. The revolutionists, more formidable through their audacity and passions than by their numbers.

3rd. The imperialists or Bonapartists, numbering all those who had borne arms or held offices during twenty years.

4th. The indifferent, who asked but for peace, and formed the great mass of the middle classes; these constitute the most considerable por-

---

24. This sacrifice was not at all to his character, and we doubt if he would have submitted to it; but after all, this was only feasible previous to the declaration. But in the month of May, after the additional act, it was impossible.

tion of the nation,

The facility of Napoleon's triumph arose from the fact, that the last three classes had declared in his favour; but the masses only act through passion or interest: as soon as it was evident that the sole fact of his presence was to lead to a general war, the numerous classes of the indifferent rose up against him, while political acts cooled the energetic party of the revolution: henceforward the chances were not the same. He did everything in his power in the position where fate had placed him. Convinced that a Cincinnatus or a Washington could not conduct France, and fully decided on reconstituting a strong and durable government, he displeased the aspirants for the tribune and the clubs, and through them the revolutionary masses. The royalist party, increased by many of the partisans for peace at any price; and his, diminished daily by these defections.

The only resource left to the emperor, was to persuade the patriots and authorities that their cause was inseparable from his own. He could boldly tell them so, for if the nation had thought otherwise, she should have rejected the new institutions awarding him the empire, and have openly treated with Europe for the recognition of his son, or for any other government. This was the end he struggled to attain at the *Champ de Mai*. The solemn acts published at this epoch, and at the opening of the chambers, are effectively the best answers that his partisans can make to his detractors: and although details of this nature enter but little in the course of this summary, we will give a few words.

The convocation of the *Champ de Mai*, awaited with so much impatience, had certainly lost a portion of the charm with which imagination clothed it, since the additional act had provided, in rather an unexpected manner, for the most important object of this reunion. Up to that time, a semi-mythologic ceremony was anticipated, the result of which would be a return of the golden age. The multitude undoubtedly thought, that each one would have the power to furnish his article to the compact thus fabricated in open air, within this new forum.

What would be done at this assembly? was asked upon all sides: some said that the emperor would present the empress and her son, as a pledge of his reconciliation with Europe and of the duration of his dynasty; others expected wonders, at the expense of their imagination. At last, the first of June, so anxiously awaited, arrived: the ceremony took place with all possible pomp in the Champ de Mars.

Napoleon, clothed in the imperial mantle, and surrounded by his dethroned brothers, and the doctrinaire Lucien, by grand functionaries, marshals, and many prelates, was seated on a superb throne erected near the military school. Twenty thousand electors seated on benches, forming an amphitheatre, constituted the first circle; farther off, were the deputies from the army: then fifty thousand soldiers, in full dress, placed behind them, and an immense population of the curious, gave a magnificent aspect to this solemnity.

Divine service having been performed, M. Dubois d'Angers pronounced an elegant address in the name of the electors of France, and proclaimed the acceptance of the additional act. Napoleon, having responded to this discourse in a firm and energetic tone, took the oath of fidelity to this charter for himself and his own; and Cambacéres, on the part of the electors, swore, *in the name of France*, fidelity of the French people to his new government. This oath was repeated spontaneously by all the electors and army deputies, in which even a large portion of the spectators joined; then followed a distribution of flags to the deputations from the army, to the troops present, and to the national guard.

However imposing this ceremony, the ideologists, political adversaries of Napoleon, saw in it but theatrical pomp; they demanded if this was the national Congress, announced with so much emphasis to give laws to the country, and if this formal preparation was necessary, in order to attend a mass, deliver a discourse, take an oath, and distribute flags. So fashionable had the spirit of defamation become, that they even ventured to say that France, tired of *coups de théâtre*, demanded things of a more serious nature.

Napoleon had however given in his address, the explanation of his conduct, in these words:

> Emperor, consul, soldier, I hold all from the French people. In prosperity, in adversity, on the battle-field, in council, on the throne, in exile, France has been the sole and constant object of my thoughts and my actions. Like the king of Athens,[25] I sacrificed myself at Fontainbleau for my people, in the hope of seeing the realization of the promise given, to preserve to France the natural integrity of her territory, her honour and

---

25. Codrus saved Athens from Heraclides, not by relinquishing his crown, but by throwing himself disguised in the midst of the enemy, in order to accomplish the sacrifice demanded by an oracle. An exile on the Isle of Elba was a sacrifice quite equivalent to an honourable death, but it was not voluntary.

her rights. The indignation at seeing these sacred rights, acquired by twenty-five years of victories, disregarded and lost forever; the cry of French honour tarnished; the wishes of the nation have recalled me to the throne, which is dear to me as being the palladium of the independence, the honour, and the rights of the people.

Frenchmen! in traversing the provinces of the empire through the midst of public rejoicing, I had reason to calculate on a long peace, because nations are bound by the treaties concluded by their governments. My thoughts were then entirely bent on the means of establishing our liberties, through a constitution conformable to the will and interest of the nation. With this object, I have convoked the *Champ de Mai*. I soon learned, however, that the kings, so often combined against us, desired to make war upon us; they think of augmenting the kingdom of the Netherlands and giving it as barriers, all our northern strongholds; and to conciliate the differences that still exist, they speak of sharing Lorraine and Alsace among themselves: it is then necessary to prepare for war.

Before personally encountering the dangers of the battle-field, my first solicitude has been to give formal existence to the nation. The people have accepted the act with which I have presented them.

When we have repelled these unjust aggressions, and Europe shall be convinced of what is due to the rights of twenty-eight millions of Frenchmen, then a solemn law, drawn up according to the forms required by the constitutional act, will unite the different dispositions of our constitutions, at present dispersed.[26]

You are about returning to your departments: say to the citizens that circumstances are of a serious nature, but that with union, energy and perseverance, we will issue victorious, from this struggle of a great people Tell them that the kings who heretofore sought my alliance, are now directing all their blows against my person. If I did not see that they aim at injuring the country,

---

26. This speech of Napoleon was wise and noble; it nevertheless displeased on account of this reticence; it held out, on the one side, the revision of the constitution as necessary, and on the other, that this revision would be in fact but a union of dispositions already existing, though scattered among many acts. Thereafter, the emperor's sincere conversion was not credited, although his language was, notwithstanding, that of a statesman, who knows how to appreciate good institutions, but who is also aware of the demands exacted by emergencies, in which a nation may be placed.

I would place at their mercy, this existence, against which they are so exasperated. But say to them also, that as long as they entertain for me sentiments of love, of which they have given me so many proofs, this hate of our enemies will be impotent. Frenchmen! my will is that of the nation, my rights are hers; my honour, my glory, my happiness, cannot be but the honour, the glory, and the happiness of France.

This discourse, delivered in a firm and animated voice, excited the liveliest enthusiasm.

A few days afterwards, the electors left for their departments, after having proclaimed the acceptance of the additional act, and nominated deputies to the new assembly.

On the 7th June, the emperor convened the two chambers with the following address:

Three months ago, circumstances and the confidence of the French people clothed me with unlimited power. The most urgent desire of my heart is accomplished today; I perform the first act of the constitutional monarchy. Men are too powerless to secure the future, institutions alone fix the destinies of nations. Monarchy is necessary in France, to guaranty the liberty, the independence, and the rights of the people.

Our constitutions are dispersed: one of our most important occupations will be to reunite them in one body, and to arrange them with one mind. This work will recommend the present epoch to future generations. I am ambitious to see France in the enjoyment of all possible liberty: I say possible, because it is necessary to avoid anarchy, leading, as it ever does, to absolute power.

A formidable coalition of kings have a design upon our independence, her armies are on our frontier. Our enemies count on our intestine divisions. . . Some legislative measures are indispensable for the future. I confide unreservedly in your intelligence, patriotism, and attachment. The liberty of the press is inherent in our present constitution, nothing there can be altered without changing our political system; but good laws for restraining it are necessary, especially in the present condition of the nation: I recommend this important object to your consideration.

The first duty of a prince will soon call me to head the children of France The army and myself will do our duty. Do you, peers and representatives, give the nation an example of confidence, energy and patriotism. Like the senate of the great people of antiquity, resolve to die rather than survive the dishonour and the degradation of France: the holy cause of the country will be triumphant.

The chambers voted separate addresses: both dwelt on the necessity of subjecting absolute power to constitutional forms and rules. They moreover promised, in the event of a reverse, to exhibit perseverance, and redouble their attachment to the imperial cause, which was the cause of France. The peers assured Europe, that with the new institutions, the allurements of victory would not lead the chief of state beyond the bounds of prudence. This was a recrimination on the past, to which Napoleon answered:

The struggle in which we are engaged is a serious one; the temptation of prosperity is not the danger which now threatens us; foreigners wish to force us under the Caudine forks. The justice of our cause, the public spirit of the nation, and the courage of the army, are powerful reasons for our hoping success. But if we experience reverses, it is then especially that I should love to see all the energy of this great people displayed. Then it is that I should find in the chamber of peers, proofs of attachment to the country and her chief. It is in trying times that great nations, like great individuals, show forth all the energy of their character, and become objects of admiration to posterity.

This posterity will acknowledge, while perusing these words, that the emperor neglected nothing in his power, to raise France to a level with the dangers that threatened her, and all of which he had foreseen. His answer to the chamber of deputies proves it still more conclusively.

This chamber, resting on the promise of properly arranging the constitutional laws, did not dissimulate its impatience to leap at once into this slippery arena.

Faithful to its mission, it will fulfil (it said) the task devolved upon it in this noble work: it demands that, in order to satisfy the public wishes, the national deliberation shall rectify, without delay, what the urgency of our situation has produced defective or left imperfect in the ensemble of our institutions. *And while your majesty opposes the honour of our national arms and the power of your genius to this most unjust aggression, the chamber of representatives will endeavour to attain the same end, by labouring without relaxation on the compact, the perfection of which should continue to cement the union of the people and the throne, and by the amelioration of our institutions, strengthen in the eyes of Europe the guaranty of our engagements*

This plainly announced the idea of taking advantage of the emperor's absence, for publicly establishing constitutional controversies, without awaiting the initiative of the government, which, nevertheless, constituted the fundamental basis of the national existence. This was going back to the constituent assembly of 1789, under still more dangerous circumstances: this was, in a word, a revolutionary act, since by one single stroke it changed the face of the government.

These discourses attest, on the one side, that the additional act was not considered the last say of Napoleon; but they also proved that he would undoubtedly have to sustain more than one assault from these men, who persisted in viewing the government as a public enemy, unceasingly thinking on the means of chaining its authority, so as to reduce its sphere of action to the most perfect nullity possible. A frightful misconception, which will forever be a certain index of the decay of a state, or the signal of anarchy.

Though Napoleon appreciated these phrases to their just value, he exhibited moderation in applauding the intentions of doctrinaires, and limiting himself to calling their attention to the dangers of untimely controversies. His answer should find a place here, as it completes the picture of his position and that of his antagonists. "Under these painful circumstances, my mind is absorbed by the imminent war, to the success of which are attached the honour and independence of France. Tonight I will depart to place myself at the head of my armies During my absence, I will take pleasure in seeing a commission, appointed by each chamber, maturely deliberating on our institutions: the constitution is our rallying point, it should be our polar star in these stormy times.

"But all possible discussion, tending to diminish, directly or indirectly, the confidence that should be reposed in the government and its dispositions, would be a misfortune to the state: we would find ourselves in the midst of dangers, without guide and without direction. The crisis at which we have arrived is a perilous one: let us not imitate the example of the Lower Empire, which, when pressed on all sides by the barbarians, rendered herself the laughing-stock of posterity, by attending to abstract discussions, at the very moment the enemy's battering-ram burst open the gates of the capital."

Prophetic words, and well calculated to confound all those declaimers who, forgetful of the emperor's principles at this memorable epoch, have levelled so many blows against him.

Napoleon thus plainly perceived, that the measures to which he had to a certain extent been compelled to have recourse, so as to satisfy public opinion, were producing a deplorable effect: they soon aimed at words instead of things, at stormy discussions instead of calm and quiet administration, and at a later period, led to divisions in the state, through authority arrogated to themselves by the chambers. It was already perceived that the concessions, however extended, still found detractors. At a moment, when the liberty of the press should have been deferred till the country was free from danger, the emperor was obliged to solicit restraining laws for diminishing its abuse, and even this step was presented as a tendency to despotism. Pamphlets of every hue, written by demagogues, others by emigrants, attacked all the measures of government, and impaired that confidence by which it was more than ever necessary it should be encircled. License was carried to such ex- cess, that sheets recommending the attempt and promising deification to those who would, by any means whatever, deliver France from the yoke of Napoleon, did not find juries to condemn them.

Scarcely was he seated on the throne, when he was forced to regret not having simply seized a discretionary power, by proclaiming himself dictator of the French empire, and abolishing all organic laws as well as the new investiture of the imperial title, until peace had been restored.

Nevertheless, if these concessions, far from satisfying the factions, clothed them with more importance, we must own that the enthusiasm excited by his promises to the party of the revolution, was not without its advantages; for, besides the national guards, whose levying it facilitated, it gave means for arming the people of the principal cities. Those of Paris alone formed twenty battalions of *tirailleurs féderés*, troops undoubtedly not very formidable in an open field, but which, when distributed in garrisons, might in case of need serve as a lever for the government in the execution of great national measures, and also contribute in the defence of cities. Fouché and Carnot, who in concert directed all the affairs of the interior, exhibited, perhaps with a different object, great ardour in the organization of these patriotic federations; both saw in them a means of counteracting the influence of the army, and consequently the authority of its chief. With the power of disposing of all the interior forces, they would be more powerful than he during the war, and would not much fear him after the peace. The first especially, who had more address and greater grasp of mind, saw in these elements a means of getting rid of Napoleon without welcoming the Bourbons, as little as the success of the struggle with Europe seemed doubtful.

Napoleon was too clear-sighted and distrustful not to suspect these projects; but he was obliged to submit to the best circumstances.

While these cares of internal policy painfully occupied his thoughts, he had redoubled his activity in his military preparations, so as to place himself in a condition to resist all Europe, should the nation, seriously appreciating her position, desire to make every sacrifice for the maintenance of her independence. The armouries, abandoned under his predecessor, resumed such activity, that they succeeded in fabricating four thousand muskets per day. The national guards *mobile* were organized throughout the empire, at the same time that the conscription was levied. I have already stated that the line of the army had been doubled in two months, (from 1st April to the 1st June), and that a vast system of defence would permit its increase to 700,000 men by the 1st September.

The problem of French independence depended, then, on the possibility of delaying hostilities till the beginning of August. Far from allowing him this time, the allies, profiting by his example, hastened with all speed towards the Rhine and the Meuse. The English and Prussians showed unheard of activity in their preparations, and the Russians reached the banks of the Rhine from the depths of Poland, in two months. The allies who were contending for Saxony arid Cracow had remained under arms with a war complement, they had lighted matches, and twenty minutes' time, with four orders for the march dispatched from Vienna the same day, were only necessary to place the whole of Europe in motion.

France was far from presenting the formidable attitude that Europe had preserved; everything was in confusion; on the arrival of Napoleon, she was without arms and without soldiers. They have tried to establish a parallel between her efforts in 1793 and those in 1815: in less time, Napoleon had accomplished as much as the committee of public safety, without having recourse to the revolutionary army, nor to a dozen guillotines that followed: but the members of the coalition of 1815 acted very differently from those of the first invasion; they did not spend three months in besieging Valenciennes, as Mack and Cobourg did; times were very much changed. The sea was covered with English convoys bearing troops and siege equipages. The riches of Hindostan, seconded by proficiency in the arts and manufactures, had transformed England into an immense arsenal, that fabricated, with terrible activity, the artillery, munitions and trains necessary to the armies of the coalition. Nothing in the most distant times resembled this epoch.

Since the last of May, Wellington and Blucher had assembled 220,000 English, Prussians, Belgians, Hanoverians and Brunswickers, between Liège and Courtray. The troops of Bavaria, Wirtemburg and Baden assembled in the Black Forest and in the Palatinate. The Austrians hastened to join them: their army of Italy was reunited at Sardes, on the Alps. The Russians, by forced marches, were already traversing Franconia and Saxony. A million of men, in short, were preparing to rush upon France: it may be said, that the coalition had the secret of Cadmus, for making soldiers spring forth from the bowels of the earth.

Whatever might be the activity employed in reorganizing the army, and in the defence of the frontier, Napoleon must have feared that the armies of Europe would be much greater than his own, should hostilities commence before the month of August. It was then under the walls of Paris and Lyons, that the destinies of the empire were to be decided.

More than once he had had the idea of fortifying the heights of Paris; but was prevented by the fear of alarming the country and by the emergencies that were thickening around him. There were two methods of effecting this; the first was by constructing seven or eight large forts on the principal points of this enceinte; if these forts did not absolutely prevent their penetrating to the walls, and even forcing an entrance into the city, it would require a very considerable force to make the attempt, for fear there still existed a nucleus of a French army that might take part in the defence. Besides this, by commanding the navigation of the Seine and closing the principal avenues, they would render the provisioning of Paris by the enemy who dared to hold it, a very difficult matter. Lastly, these forts might be connected by communicating intrenchments.

The other method was to place the entire *encernte* under protection from a *coup de main*, by means of field works. The emperor gave this the preference because it required less time. He thought that a great capital contains the elite of the nation, that it is the centre of opinion, the depot of everything, and that it is the greatest inconsistency to leave so important a point without immediate defence. In times of misfortunes and great calamities, states are often in want of actual soldiers, but never in want of men for the defence of their walls. Fifty thousand national guards with two or three thousand cannoniers, will defend a fortified capital against an army of 200,000 men. These 50,000 men in an open field, if not disciplined soldiers and commanded by experienced officers, will be routed by a charge of a few thousand horse.

Paris has often owed her safety to her walls; if in 1814 she had been in condition to resist but for eight days, what influence would this not have had on the events of the world? If in 1805, Vienna had been well armed and better defended, the Battle of Ulm had not decided the war; Austerlitz had never been fought. If in 1806, Berlin had been fortified, the army beaten at Jéna had rallied, and the Russian army would have joined it. If in 1808, Madrid had been fortified, the French army after the victories of Espinosa, Tudela, Burgos, and Sommo-Sierra, had not dared to march on this capital, leaving the English and Spanish armies behind them, towards Salamanca and Valladolid. Lastly, it was the fortifications of Vienna, that on two occasions saved Europe from the sabre of the Mussulman.

General Haxo was consequently charged with fortifying Paris. This skilful engineer, intrenched the heights situated on the north from Montmartre to Charonne, and completed the Ourcq canal, so as to cover the plain between La-Villette and St. Denis. This village was to be intrenched and protected by the inundations of the Rouillon and the Crou. From the western foot of Montmartre ran a line of intrenchments that rested on the Seine above Clichy: at the eastern extremity, the Bercy park and the space between Vincennes and Charonne were equally covered. The works were armed with 700 pieces of ordnance. On the south, the faubourgs between the upper Seine and la Bièvre and between la Bièvre and the lower Seine, were not to remain without defence; their *enceinte* had been already traced out when the enemy appeared before Paris.

General Léry presided over the defensive works at Lyons; they were pushed with vigour: 450 iron pieces of heavy calibre brought from Toulon, and 250 bronze pieces, armed the ramparts or were kept in reserve. Everything led to the belief that the inhabitants of this city, whose patriotism equals their courage, supported by a *corps d'armée*, would give the enemy a task.

While these great works were being executed, recruiting was carried on with all the possible activity that circumstances would permit. It will be remembered that by the 1st June the effectives of the line of the army had been increased from 200,000 to 400,000 men; but in this number must be included the soldiers who were still at the regimental depots, as well as the forces required in the west, on the southern frontier, and in the most important fortresses of the empire. Napoleon had then 180,000 disposable men for the campaign on the Rhine and in Belgium. By the middle of July, he would have had 300,000; all the forts would, moreover, have had garrisons of national guards, depots for the line, and some good regiments.[27]

All the efforts to enter upon negotiations having been vain, Napoleon had the option to pursue one of two courses; the first, to meet the Anglo-Prussians at Brussels or Namur, about the middle of June; the second, to await the allies at Paris and Lyons. The latter had the inconvenience of delivering half of France to the ravages of the enemy; but it offered the advantage of gaining until the month of August to finish recruiting and complete the preparations, then of fighting with all his means combined while the allies were weakened by many corps of observation. On the contrary, by transporting the theatre of hostilities into Belgium, France was perhaps saved from invasion; but in case of reverse the allies would be drawn on by the 1st July, six weeks earlier than they would have come of their own accord.[28]

The *armée d'élite*, shaken by a reverse, would no longer be able to sustain so unequal a struggle, and the recruiting might not be com-

---

27. The troops of the line had been augmented in two months, from 200,000 to 360,000 men; but 150,000 were not yet disposable, being in depots. Besides these, there were 200,000 complete, comprising the national guard mobile, which would not be fit for service before the end of July, though by the middle of June they might be already assembled in the fortresses. By the end of August Napoleon expected to have from seven to eight hundred thousand defenders at his disposal. Immense works were ordered for putting in order all the frontier places, for a long time neglected, and especially to fortify Paris, Lyons, Laone, Soissons, and the mountain passes.

28. This calculation, that might very naturally enter into Napoleon's thoughts, being based on the inarch of the Russian armies, the farthest off of all, was not exact, as to time, because the coalesced power had taken measures for entering France at all points on the 1st July. This was, besides, an additional motive for anticipating them in Belgium, if in condition to do so.

pleted. On the other hand, this course offered the hope of taking the enemy unawares; it was more conformable with the spirit of the nation that does riot comprehend Fabius. This method can be acted upon by an emperor of. Russia, with an endless empire; or by a Wellington on the territory of another beyond the sea; but in a country like France whose capital is seventy leagues from the Belgian frontier, and in the position which the emperor was personally placed, the idea of permitting Europe in arms to reach the base of Montmartre, would have terrified the most determined.

Undoubtedly, if France had had but one feeling and one will, that of rallying around the chief of state and conquering with him, it would perhaps have been better to await the enemy. But with existing divisions in political interests, opinions, and passions, everything was to be dreaded while awaiting an invasion; because with the impossibility of making head at all points at once, he would have been constrained to deliver half of the provinces to the ravages of war, and the chamber of deputies, already so hostile to his power, would not have spared him. A victory beyond, would procure him the necessary time, and would impose silence on his political enemies in the interior: it would thus suit him in every respect; for in beating Wellington and Blucher separately, he delivered himself from the dangers he foresaw on the part of Fouché and Carnot. Moreover, he has unevasively avowed that he believed himself certain of this victory, while perceiving the enthusiasm of the soldiers and recurring to the souvenirs of the past.

All these motives determined him then to take the initiative, not to occupy Brussels, but to destroy the opposing masses in succession. If he succeeded, the defeat of Wellington and Blucher ought to be followed by important consequences; this great blow struck apropos at the opening of the campaign, might dissolve the coalition. Meanwhile, it was impossible to garrison the other points of the frontier: it was necessary to leave small bodies at Bordeaux, Toulouse, on the Var, in Savoy, at Béfort, and Strasbourg. These bodies, too feeble to resist in front of an enemy, were to serve at least for awing and harassing him on the march: moreover these were *points d'appui*, valuable for levying the national guards, and for the rising of the country which they were to organize.

To increase the misfortune, la Vendée was not quieted, notwithstanding the success of the movable columns. Civil war is a political cancer which should be destroyed in its germ, under pain of compromising the safety of the state; even a portion of the young guard had to be sent to re-enforce the corps of General Lamarque. All these detachments reduced the strength of the main army to 120,000 combatants, which were to assemble between the Meuse and the Sambre, from Philippeville to Maubeuge.

Although the enemy had at least 200,000 men in Belgium, Napoleon did not hesitate; it was important not to lose time, so as to avoid having on his hands all the hostile armies at once. Leaving Paris on the 12th June, he inspected the armament of Soissons and Laon the next day, and on the 14th removed his headquarters to Beaumont.

The organization of the army underwent great modifications: the emperor gave the command of corps to young generals who, called upon to win their marshal's baton on the battlefield, would exhibit more enthusiasm for the triumph of his cause. This baton was conferred on Grouchy, who had shown talent and vigour in the campaign of 1814, and in his expedition against the Duke d'Angoulême. Soult was appointed major-general in place of Berthier, who had forsaken his flag to follow the Bourbons, and who it is said, threw himself from the casement of the palace of Bamberg, ashamed of finding himself in the midst of the enemy's columns that defiled before him en route for the frontier of France.[29] Davoust remained as minister of war, Mortier was to command the guard; but his health did not permit it. Ney and Grouchy were to conduct the wings of the main army, in the quality of lieutenants. Suchet commanded the army of Italy, Rapp on the Rhine, Brune on the Var, Clausel and Decaen watched the Pyrenees.

Napoleon had four lines of operation from which to choose; he could reunite his masses on the left towards Valenciennes, pounce by Mons, on Brussels, fall upon the English army and overthrow it on Antwerp. By the centre he could act on Charleroi, through Maubeuge, between the Sambre and the Meuse, and fall on the point of junction of the two armies of Blucher and Wellington. On the right he could descend the Meuse towards Namur, fall on the left of the Prussians, cutting them off from Coblentz and Cologne. Lastly, it was possible to make a descent between the Meuse and the Moselle, or between the Meuse and the Rhine, fall on the corps of Kleist that covered the Ardennes, and the communications of the Prussians with the Rhine.

---

29. Berthier's death is still covered by a veil of mystery; the fact is, he fell from the balcony on to the pavement. Some say he was thrown by the son of a bookseller of Nuremberg, who had been condemned to death under the empire; others think, that the spectacle of the Russian army defiling on their way to enter France, made him regret his having emigrated.

This last course led only to threatenings, that would have resulted in nothing with a man of Blucher's character. Besides, it led too far from the end intended. An attack on the Meuse was most wise, but it would have thrown Blucher on Wellington, and effected the junction that should be prevented. The inverse manoeuvre by Mons against Wellington's army, might have produced in an opposite manner the same dreaded junction, by throwing the right of the allies upon the left. The emperor at last determined on falling upon the central point, where he might take Blucher *en flagrant délit*, and defeat him before he could receive the support of Wellington.

In order properly to appreciate its merit, it must be remembered that Napoleon had not to oppose only one army, under the same chief, and having but one interest, but on the contrary, two armies independent of each other, having two bases of operations entirely diverging: that of the English being based on Ostend, or Antwerp, and that of the Prussians on the Rhine and Cologne; decisive circumstances, and which secured great success to all central operations, tending to separate them and fight them successively.

Napoleon's taking the field, and his first plan, may be regarded as among the most remarkable operations of his life: nine corps of infantry or cavalry cantoned from Lille to Metz, were, by marches skilfully concealed, to concentrate in front of Charleroi, at the same moment with the guard's arrival there from Paris. These movements were combined with so much precision, that 120,000 men were assembled on the Sambre, as by enchantment, on the 14th June. Wellington, occupied in giving fêtes at Brussels, believed Napoleon still in Paris, when his columns presented themselves on the morning of the 15th to cross this river. The French troops occupied over night the following positions: the right, 16,000 strong, under Count Gérard, at Philippeville; the centre, nearly 60,000 strong, under Napoleon, towards Beaumont; and the left, 45,000 strong, at Ham-sur-Eur and Solre-sur-Sambre.

The enemy had such slight idea of these movements that their armies were not concentrated. Blucher had the first of his corps at Charleroi, the second at Namur, the third at Dinant, and the fourth under Bulow, at Liège; the fifth under Kleist, covered Luxembourg. Meanwhile, Napoleon learned on joining his army, that General Bourmont had deserted on the 14th, from Philippeville, to join Louis XVIII. and the allies. However censurable this step might be, it may be believed, that it was not aggravated, by giving the enemy such information as a soldier should conceal even in such a case.

At all events, under the circumstances, when endeavouring to surprise them in their cantonments, the mere knowledge of the emperor's arrival and the assembling of his army, was a serious matter; this information sufficed for Blucher to order the concentration of his corps, and thus counteracting all plans for a surprise. We are, however, assured that he had already ordered this assembling, on previous advices received through a drummer of the old guard who had deserted that night; the presence of the old guard was a certain index, and sufficient to warn the enemy.

As to Wellington's army, it had not yet stirred from the cantonments it occupied from Oudinarde, on l'Escaut to Nivelle: but it had been apprised and was ready to do so at the first signal.

The events were so important and so hurried in this campaign of four days, that I will be obliged to enter into details to have it understood, and to insert in this place, a table of the situations of the respective armies on the morning of the 15th, to accomplish the same object. If Napoleon did not then know precisely the composition and position of all the enemy's corps, he at least knew that in general terms, the Prussians cantoned from Charleroi to Liège, and that the Anglo-Belgians were distributed between Ath and Brussels, with advanced guards towards Mons and Tournay. The point of junction of these two armies, was then on the causeway leading from Charleroi to Brussels, and it was there also that he directed his blows, with the greater hope of being able to profit thus by the dissemination of the enemy's forces, and overthrow them separately.

As success depended on celerity, the French army crossed the frontier on the 15th at dawn, and took the direction of Charleroi. The corps of General Reille, that bivouacked at Ham-sur-Eur, being nearest the enemy, was to cross the Sambre at Marchiennes, and march on Gosselies: that of d'Erlon which was farther to the rear at Solre-sur-Sambre, was to follow the same direction. The centre or main body, with the cavalry reserves under Grouchy,[30] marched from Beaumont on Charleroi, and the right from Philippeville upon Catelet, where it was to cross the Sambre, cutting off the Prussian division that held Charleroi, from its retreat on Namur.

These movements though partly unforeseen by the enemy, did not entirely attain their object. Reille's corps actually crossed the Sambre

---

30. Under this first organization, Grouchy commanded all the cavalry; it was only on the morrow, the 16th June, that the army was organized into two wings, and that he took command of the right.

SITUATION OF THE FRENCH ARMY, JUNE 14th, 1815.

ARMY ON ACTIVE SERVICE IN BELGIUM.

			Str'gth	Position.
1st Corps. *Count D'Erlon.*	4 Infantry divisions : Gayot, Donzelot, Marcognet, Durutte.		20,000	Saire-sur Sambre.
	1 Cavalry do. Jacquinot.			
2d Corps. *Count Reille.*	4 Infantry do. Rebelin, Foy, Jerome Bonaparte, Girard.		22,800	Han-sur Ear.
	1 Cavalry do. Piré.			
3d Corps.	3 Infantry do. Habert, Berthezène, Lefol.		16,000	Beaumont.
Count *Vandamme.*	1 Cavalry do. Watin.			
4th Corps. *Count Gérard.*	3 Infantry do. Vichery, Petheux, Huiot.		14,000	Philippeville.
	1 Cavalry do. Morin.			
6th Corps. *Count Lobau.*	3 Infantry do. Simmer, Jeannin, Teste.		12,000	Beaumont.
	1 Cavalry do. Domon.			
Guard.	{the Old Guard, Friant & Morand............ 8,000		18,400	do.
	{2 divisions : Young Guard Duhesme 4,000			
	Cavalry of the Guard, 19 squadrons of light, and 13 of heavy cavalry. ... 4,000			
	Artillery, Sappers............ 2,400			

CAVALRY RESERVE.

		Str'gth	Position.
1st Light Corps. *Gen. Pajol.*	Soult's & Subervie's divisions of Hussars and Chasseurs.........	2,800	do.
2d Corps. *Exelmans.*	Divisions of Dragoons, Strolz & Chastel.........	3,000	do.
3d Corps. *Milhaud.*	Divisions of Cuirassiers, Watier & Delort.........	3,600	do.
4th Corps. *Count de Valmy.*	Divisions of Cuirassiers, Sheritier & Roussel.........	3,700	do.
		120,300	Combatants.

Total, 167 small battalions, 166 squadrons, 346 cannon.

OTHER TROOPS.

Rapp, commanding the army of the Rhine.
Bélard, commanding one corps at Metz.
Lecourbe, a small corps of observation at Befort.
Suchet, the army of Italy in Savoy.

Brune, the corps of observation on the Var.
Decaen and *Clausel*, the corps of observation of the Pyrenees.
Lamarque, the corps of La Vendée.

SITUATION OF THE ALLIED ARMIES IN BELGIUM, JUNE 14th, 1815.

1st. Prussians, under Marshal Blucher.

		Strength	Position
1st Corps. Zieten.	4 divisions of Infantry (*), Steinmetz, Pirch 2d, Jagow and Henkel. Röder's Cavalry, 3,000	32,800	On the Sambre, at Thuin & Auvelny.
2d Corps. Pirch.	4 divisions of Infantry: Tippels, Kirch, Krafft, Brause and Langen. Jurgas' Cavalry, 4,000	31,800	About Namur.
3d Corps. Thielmann.	4 divisions of Infantry: Borcke, Kempfen, Luck and Stulpnagel. Hobe's Cavalry, 2,400	24,000	About Ciney and Dinant.
4th Corps. Bülow.	4 divisions of Infantry: Hacke, Ryssel, Losin and Hiller. Prince William of Prussia's Cavalry, 3,000	30,300	Near Liege.
5th Corps. Kleist.	Nearly 30,000		Luxembourg, Bastoché.

Total, not including *Kleist*, 136 battalions, 135 squadrons, 320 cannon............ 118,900 Combatants.

2d. Army of Anglo-Netherlanders, under the Duke of Wellington.

		Strength	Position
1st Corps. Prince of Orange.	(2 English divisions, the Guards and Alten's. 10,800		Enghien, Sohne and environs.
	Dutch Belgian Army; The Indian Brigade, Bierman's division. 24,300		Oudenarde and Nivelle.
	General Collaert's Cavalry. 4,600		Braine le Compt, Ath, Remit, Oudinarde, Leuze, Brussels.
2d Corps. General Hill.	3 divisions Anglo-Hanoverians, Clinton, Coleville, Picton, Lambert and Decken, without the Artillery.	34,000	
Corps of Brunswick: Infantry and Cavalry.		9,930	Ghent and Mons, Brussels, Malines.
Contingent from Nassau		6,730	
Artillery		3,000	do. Genape.
		6,000	

Total, 123 battalions, 114 squadrons, 230 cannon................ 90,360 Combatants.

Total of the two armies, not including *Kleist* and some garrisons, 550 cannon..... 218,800 Combatants.

OTHER TROOPS.

The Grand Austro-Russian army, under Barclay de Tolly and Schwarzenberg, were assembling on the Rhine with the Bavarians and Würtembergers, upwards of............................ 350,000

The Austro-Sardinians in Italy, The Swiss, Spaniards and small German contingents increased the allied force to 820,000 or 830,000 men............ 100,000

(*) The Prussians called these *brigades*, but they were stronger than the French divisions: they had 40 batteries and Wellington had 51. I have estimated them at 8 pieces each, as an average.

successfully, and gained the route to Gosselies, preceded by the light cavalry of the guard; but Gérard's leaving Philippeville, having a much longer march to execute, and over detestable roads, arrived at Catelet too late to gain the road to Gilly, and fulfil its destination.

The centre had, also, very execrable roads to traverse, in running over from Beaumont to Charleroi, and Vandamme, who should have formed the head of this column, was rather late in leaving his camp.[31] The Prussian generals, whose divisions were parcelled out on the line, had thus more leisure in assembling them and evacuating Charleroi, this being in their plan of concentration; only two or three battalions were cut to pieces in the partial combats. The first division of Ziethen's corps, wishing to retreat from Piéton through Gosselies, and finding this point already occupied by Reille's advanced guard, had to force its way in order to reach Heppignies. The second division reassembled at Gilly on the Namur road. Reille's corps having driven the Prussian division from Gosselies, and perceiving it continuing the retreat by Heppignies upon Fleurus, Girard's division was ordered to follow, while the other three divisions continued their march upon Frasne. The light cavalry of the guard that preceded it, drove from this borough the advanced guard of Prince Weimar, who concentrated his brigade on Quatre-Bras.

Grouchy's light cavalry having debouched from Charleroi upon Gilly, found there Ziethen's two divisions, and was obliged to halt and await Vandamme's infantry, who were advancing with difficulty by the bridge of this city. In this position the two parties exchanged a few cannon shot.

While these French columns debouched by the bridges on the Sambre and sought the enemy, Napoleon established himself in front of Charleroi at the fork of the roads leading to Gosselies and Fleurus, where he awaited reports, and meditated on the employment to be given to the masses he had assembled with so much skill, and on the direction necessary to assign them.

Before proceeding further, it will be well to cast a *coup d'œil* on the preventive measures the allies had taken against the storm that was bursting upon them. If their generals were caught at fault at the instant of the irruption, it must be acknowledged that they were actually well

---

31. General Gourgaud will have it thus; but we have reason to believe that an error was committed in transmitting the orders, for Vandamme was not one of those men whose activity must be stimulated; he was but too ardent, unless some personal jealousy had excited his displeasure.

prepared for whatever might happen. The Anglo-Prussians desired to assume the offensive on the 1st July; during the interval they had adopted all the precautions necessary, in case they were anticipated. All the partial and general concentrations were properly indicated. They understood Napoleon's system of piercing divided centres too well, not to foresee that he would manoeuvre in order to separate the two armies. Under this hypothesis, Blucher had chosen the position in rear of Ligny for assembling on his right, and Wellington had selected Quatre-Bras for concentrating on his left; meanwhile he had reconnoitred the position between Hall and Mont-Saint-Jean (or Waterloo,) for covering Brussels, and there to accept battle, if the French either debouched by Valenciennes and Mons, or arrived by Charleroi.

These dispositions were incontestably wise, but with the impetuosity and ordinary vivacity of the enterprises and the movements of the emperor of the French, they might yet fail in accomplishing their object and be separated.

After what had been agreed upon, as soon as Blucher heard at Namur of the approach of the imperial army, he dispatched at midnight of the 14th, orders to Ziethen to fall back, fighting on Fleurus; prescribed at the same time the assembling of Pirch's corps at Sombref; ordered Thielmann to march in all haste from Dinant to Namur, while Bulow should concentrate on Hanut. These measures, evidently suggested by the reports of deserters, denoted however that Blucher calculated on a hasty crossing of the Sambre, and on a decisive battle for the morrow.

Napoleon could not as yet understand all these circumstances; but after the varied information he had received, and from the direction of the retreat of the Prussian forces, he perceived that their army sought to assemble between Namur and the causeway leading from Charleroi to Brussels, as it was by this route that the English would come to their assistance: now, under this supposition the emperor had but one wise course to follow; the most simple glance at the map would sufficiently indicate, that it was essential to seize upon Sombref on the one side, and the central point of Quatre-Bras on the other. (A village that took its name from the intersection of two roads, forming four branches, leading to Namur, Charleroi, Brussels and Nivelles.) Because, once master of these two points, he was in position to act at will on either of the opposing armies, and prevent their junction.

Consequently, Napoleon gave Grouchy a verbal order, to push as far as Sombref that very evening, if possible: Marshal Ney, who had just arrived by post from Paris, was ordered to assume command of the left wing, composed of Reille's and Erlon's corps, to take at once the Brussels road, in the direction of Quatre-Bras, and push forward advanced guards on the three branches that parted from that point, to gather every information.[32]

Having learned at that moment, that Grouchy's cavalry had been arrested near Gilly by a portion of Ziethen's corps, Napoleon hastened there to order an attack; the enemy observing the arrival of Vandamme's infantry, retired, fighting, and after quite a brisk cannonade, Excelmans and Vandamme dislodged him from the woods of Soleilmont and Larnbusart, where Ziethen's third division had collected.

While this was taking place, Marshal Key arrived between Gosselies and Frasne, and hearing the booming of cannon in the direction of Gilly during the attack of Ziethen's second division by Vandamme and Grouchy, believed that this engagement might modify the emperor's designs, and therefore, instead of briskly pushing forward as far as Quatre-Bras, he established himself in front of Gosselies. This *contre-temps* was the more grievous, as in admitting that Ney had not received a formal order, he should have felt the importance of this occupation. It has been said in his justification, that his troops, especially those of d'Erlon's corps that had advanced from Solre over frightful roads, were still scattered between Gosselies and Marchiennes; it has been added that the roar of artillery in rear of his right flank, induced the belief that his recall might become necessary, and that his march should not be continued for fear of having too much road to travel in retracing his steps[33]: Bachelu's division, that had been thrown forward

---

32. This fact, asserted in Gourgaud's account, is contested by Ney's defenders. It is certain that in the orders written by Soult, no trace of this movement is found till the morning of the 16th; but it is also certain that Napoleon gave Ney, on the night of the 15th, all the instructions *verbally*, as well as to Grouchy, whom he ordered to push on as far as Sombref if possible. It is then more than probable that he gave Ney, by word of mouth, the order cited by Gourgaud with circumstances that do not permit a doubt. How, in fact, would he have pushed his right as far as Sombref, leaving his left in rear at Gosselies, when this wing had less distance to traverse, even if it had advanced as far as Quatre-Bras? Besides, if the execution of the movement seemed difficult on the night of the 15th, it is evident that it was indispensable to march on this important point at 6 the next morning.

33. We should observe, once for all, that without wishing to prejudice in the slightest degree, the faults imputed to his lieutenants, by Napoleon, we should recall his exact words used at the very moment of the catastrophe. Ney was less active and less impetuous during the 15th and 16th June than he had been at Elchingen, Jéna and Friedland; but we must take into consideration (continued next page).

as far as Frasne, was even ordered to fall back.

Be this as it may, night having set in before the right could reach Sombref, as he had desired, Napoleon probably attached less importance to the delays experienced by his left, and returned to Charleroi about 10 o'clock that night, where Ney repaired at a later hour, undoubtedly by invitation, to determine on the operations for the morrow. The troops of the main body and the cavalry, bivouacked between the woods of Lambusart and the village of Heppignies, now held by Girard's division of Reille's corps: the guard and Lobau's corps, in reserve, about Charleroi, where were fixed the imperial quarters. The corps of Count Gérard remained in the vicinity of Catelet: that of d'Erlon did not go beyond Jumet.

From all that has been stated, we see that Napoleon had to renounce the idea of pushing, on the 15th, as far as Sombref and Quatre-Bras, which were to be the pivots of all his after movements. But to secure the success of his wisely combined plan, it behooved him to repair with activity and promptness, at daybreak on the 16th, what had been left incomplete the night previous; unfortunately for him, this was not executed with that uncommon activity that ordinarily distinguished him. We are forced to avow that the manner in which he employed this morning of the 16th, will ever remain a problem for those who best understand it: did he calculate that Ney and Grouchy would themselves execute at sunrise, the verbal orders received, to advance upon Sombref and Quatre-Bras, and did he believe in his power of employing this time, in arranging the numberless affairs that besieged him at his headquarters? We can suppose so, as the emperor that morning resolved on the definite organization of his army into two principal masses and a reserve: Grouchy had the command of the right wing, composed of Vandamme's and Gérard's corps, with Pajol's, Excelmans' and Milhaud's corps of cavalry. Ney commanded the left wing, composed of Reille's and d'Erlon's corps, with the cavalry of Count de Valmy and Lefèbre Desnouettes. Lobau's corps and the guards formed a reserve of nearly 28,000 men.[34]

---

the circumstances of the case. He arrived at Charleroi by post from Paris, without equipage and even without horses, when he was immediately ordered to take command of eight divisions of infantry he had never seen, of which he scarcely knew any of the chiefs, and the positions of which were a mystery to him. Had Ney's wing have been under his orders a few days, and had their anterior movements been directed by him, it is probable that he would have reached Quatre-Bras on the night of the 15th.

34. This organization has had its critics, because, in truth, (continued next page.)

We can also suppose, that on hearing of Blucher's presence at Namur, where he had spent the 15th, the emperor concluded that he would concentrate his different corps about that city, as it was the central point of their cantonments. He could then naturally infer, that but a portion of this army would oppose him on the 16th, and that it would suffice to take an earnest step after midday: all the measures prescribed evidently prove it; for he informed Ney in the morning that he would not resolve on a definite course till three o'clock that afternoon.[35]

Nevertheless, Napoleon resolved about 8 a. m., on sending his *aide-de-camp*, Flahaut, to Marshal Ney, to reiterate the formal order for him to march hastily on Quatre-Bras, to take up a strong position there, to reconnoitre the three roads, and to detach from thence a strong infantry division with the light cavalry of the guard, on Marbais; lastly, to form a connection with Grouchy, who, with the right wing, was advancing to take possession of Sombref. This dispatch, written by Flahaut himself under Napoleon's dictation, left by 9 o'clock, and should have been preceded by a like order given by the major general: these orders reached Gosselies only towards 11 o'clock, and as the Marshal had already left to join the advance guard of Reille's corps, near Frasne, he did not immediately receive them.

While these things were happening at the imperial quarters, Grouchy's troops advanced to drive Ziethen's rear-guard from Fleurus. The latter made no opposition, but assembled on the main body, formed on the heights between Ligny and Saint Amand, in presence of which the French found themselves about eleven o'clock.

---

the army had no centre; they have thought that it had been preferable to draw the fourth division of the two corps of Reille and d'Erlon, and join them to Lobau's corps, thus forming a centre and two wings independently of the reserves; this would have facilitated the movements, and perhaps avoided the false employment of too great detachments during the 16th and 18th June. Napoleon was undoubtedly determined by the reason, that having to encounter two armies quite distinct, it behooved him to have a certain mass ready to oppose to each of them, besides the reserve to reinforce the point where he would desire to strike a blow; a result he would have attained better, by having had three masses beside the reserve.

35. This circumstance is so much the more surprising, as Grouchy had transmitted a report, at 6 a. m., announcing that the Prussians were debouching from Sombref on St. Amand in considerable forces. As this did not at all accord with the information received of Blucher's presence at Namur, Napoleon seems not to have credited it; besides, he was pained and much disturbed at the turn taken at Paris by the Chambers and Jacobins. It was not till three o'clock that he determined on a course then inexecutable.

A few moments afterwards Napoleon arrived on the spot, proceeded to reconnoitre the position, when he was informed that Ney still thought it his duty to slacken his march on Quatre-Bras, for many reasons: first, d'Erlon's corps was still very far to the rear; second, false reports that the junction of the enemy's armies had already taken place, and that therefore, the movement prescribed, far from being useful, would only prove adventurous: the marshal, therefore, awaited the emperor's decision after the receipt of this information, before seriously engaging.[36]

While this remissness threatened the success of this beautiful plan of Napoleon, the allies displayed an uncommon activity, and the Prussians especially, reassembled with rare celerity. Being informed at Namur, at 10 a. m. of the 15th, of the passage of the Sambre and the danger that menaced Ziethen, Blucher had ordered Thielmann and Bulow to march immediately on Sombref. Pirch's corps had left Namur on the 15th for this destination, and marched part of the night; Thielmann's, on their way from Dinant, had made but one halt of three hours, at Namur, to rest the troops, and had filed off the entire night towards Sombref, where the rear battalions arrived between nine and ten in the morning. Bulow, coming from Liège, could not reach Gembloux before the night of the 16th and 17th. The main body of the Prussian army (three corps, together 00,000 men) thus found itself in position between Bry and Tongrines, at ten o'clock on the morning of the 16th.

Wellington, who believed Napoleon still at Paris, was not aware of his army's approach, until the news of the passage of the Sambre received at 5 p. m., on the 15th at Brussels, while at a dinner; but the duke had forewarned his troops to hold themselves in readiness for the first signal, and he sent officers in all directions to put them in motion. His left under the Prince of Orange, was in cantonments between Mons and Nivelles, and with its headquarters at Braine le Comte; his right under General Hill, extended towards Ath. It was then only by a prodigy of activity that this extended line could be concentrated on his left by the evening of the 16th or the morning of the 17th, and it

---

36. These delays are contested by Ney's vindicators, who wish to prove that the order borne by Flahaut, not reaching Gosselies before 11 o'clock and Frasne towards noon, could not be executed before two, and that much he did. But the orders given verbally on the 15th and 16th at 1 a. m., cannot be doubted, without accusing Napoleon of incapacity. Besides, how could Ney excuse himself at nine in the morning for not having yet advanced on Quatre-Bras, if he had not previously received verbal orders.

was evident that a connection with the Prussians could be effected by the road from Nivelles to Quatre-Bras.

After having dispatched these orders, Wellington repaired to Quatre-Bras, where on the morning of the 16th he found a portion of Perpoucher's Belgian division just from Nivelles, and the brigade of the Prince of Saxe-Weimar. While awaiting the columns from Brussels and Braine, the duke galloped over to Bry, where, about noon, he held an interview with Blucher; finding the Prussian army disposed to give battle, he promised to collect thirty or thirty-five thousand men during the night, to support his right, and with this object returned to Quatre-Bras, where he arrived after two o'clock.

To conquer an enemy that made such wise dispositions, it would have required the ancient impetuosity of the conqueror of Italy, Ulm, Jéna, and Ratisbonne; but his warmest admirers would not recognize it here. As we have already observed, he undoubtedly trusted to the alacrity of his lieutenants themselves, to recover the time lost, and to execute in the morning the verbal orders he had given them the previous evening, for the occupation of two points, without which he could not reckon on the success of his project. Nevertheless this hope did not suffice, and the emperor of 1809 would not have failed being in person at Fleurus by 8 o'clock in the morning, to judge of the state of things, and to verify the report Grouchy had sent him at 6 o'clock, announcing the presence of strong Prussian columns that were debouching from Sombref on St. Amand.

Be that as it may, as we have seen above, Napoleon arrived near Fleurus at 11 o'clock, and there received information of the new delay caused in the movement on Quatre-Bras. To counteract this deplorable incident, the emperor reiterated the order to Ney, to push vigorously on Quatre-Bras, with the understanding that 8,000 men should be detached on Marbais, as soon as he received the command through General Flahaut. This new order at the same time informed him that as Grouchy was to occupy Sombref, he would certainly have to oppose but the troops hastening from Brussels. Waleski, a polish officer, was the bearer of this letter.

While the latter proceeded at a gallop on the Gosselies road, Napoleon about noon ascended the mills at Fleurus, to reconnoitre the Prussian corps whose presence had been signalled. On his front, the position was covered with difficulties that bordered the rivulet of Ligny; the left extended to the environs of Sombref and Tongrines, the centre about Ligny; the right in rear of St. Amand. This large borough, formed of three distinct villages (that bear the names of St. Amand le Château, St. Amand la Haie, and St. Amand le Hameau,) protected the right wing whose flank rested on Wagnèle. The second line and the reserves were between Sombref and Bry. Thus six large villages, four of which were difficult of access on account of the rivulet, covered the line of the enemy, like so many bastions; his reserves and his second line posted in columns of attack by battalions between Sombref and Bry, could support all points of it.[37]

After this reconnoissance, it became still more manifest that Napoleon's heaviest blow should be struck at Blucher's right; because this wing was already turned by Ney's march, and it was the only point of junction with Wellington. It is said that the emperor felt some surprise in seeing this position; all reports agreed in stating that Blucher had passed the 15th at Namur, where his army was not as yet concentrated. Though Napoleon was aware of all the interest the allies had in effecting a junction, he did not think that Blucher would thus abandon his communications with Liège and Aix-la-Chapelle, as he believed his army to be less numerous, and would have moreover expected to find it in the beautiful defensive position between Sombref and Tongrines, at the fork on the causeway from Namur. The line he had selected suited the French perfectly, but it was necessary to profit by it without delay, and too much time had already been lost.

Although this procrastination in the design on Quatre-Bras appeared vexatious, since the occupation of this point in the morning had been an important matter, we must acknowledge that after the reconnoissance just made, the emperor had cause for gratulation, as it resulted that Ney would be yet disposable in seconding his attack of the Prussians.

This reconnoissance having been completed in an hour, Napoleon had actually one of three courses to pursue:

1st. To arrest the march of Ney's column at once; order Kellermann's cavalry to take up position at Frasne, to cover the route from Charleroi, this being the line of retreat; then to throw the seven divisions of Reille's and d'Erlon's corps on Mablais, by the Roman cause-

---

37. The four divisions of Ziethen's corps formed in the front line defended Ligny and St. Amand; those of Pirch's corps forming the second line, came into line successively. The left under Thielmann, only arrived at 9 a.m., were towards Tongrines. Gourgaud's narrative states that Napoleon made this reconnoissance at 10 o'clock, while Soult, no earlier than 2 p.m., informs Ney that *a Prussian corps* has just been discovered.

way, in order to turn Blucher's right and fall upon his rear, while Napoleon attacked him in front.

2nd. To prescribe this movement for d'Erlon's corps alone, leaving Reille's corps with Kellermann's cavalry on the defensive, towards Frasne and Quatre-Bras, to watch the enemy and cover the road to Charleroi.

3rd. To direct Ney, on the contrary, to fall impetuously on all forces at Quatre-Bras, force them on Genape, in the direction of Brussels, then immediately to turn towards Bry, in the direction of Namur, and co-operate in the attack on Blucher.

In a tactical point of view, the first of these, incontestably offered the greatest results; but Napoleon had actually pushed Ney on Quatre-Bras, as much to prevent the Anglo-Belgian troops from taking the Namur road to support the Prussian army, as to cover his natural line of retreat by the road to Charleroi, and by leaving it to the protection of the cavalry alone, he relinquished this double advantage, by delivering this important route to the mercy of the enemy. Under this supposition he might have adopted the second, which had the advantage of sufficiently covering the retreat, while allowing forces sufficient to outflank Blucher's right. Napoleon preferred the third, undoubtedly with the hope that the order sent by Flahaut before 9 o'clock, would be executed at the moment this reconnoissance had been completed, and that Ney, once master of Quatre-Bras, could with so much greater security, assist in the defeat of Blucher, after having beaten the Anglo-Belgians that opposed him. However, it is probable there was some uncertainty in the emperor's resolutions, as it was not until two o'clock that the following order was sent to Ney:

In bivouac in front of Fleurus, 2 p. m.
Marshal:—The emperor instructs me to inform you, that the enemy has concentrated *a corps of troops* between Sombref and Bry, and that at half past two, Marshal Grouchy with the third and fourth corps will attack it. His majesty's intention is, that you also attack those in your front; *that after having pressed them vigorously*, you turn in this direction, and aid in enveloping the corps of which I have just spoken. If this corps is first routed, his majesty will then manoeuvre in your direction, to facilitate in a like manner your operations. You will immediately inform the emperor of your dispositions, and of what is happening in your front.

All the expressions of this dispatch seem to attest, that Napoleon was but imperfectly aware of the Prussian force, as he speaks but of *one corps*, and supposes he might be overthrown without the aid of the left wing: this last circumstance naturally explains the double interest, the French general had attached to the previous occupation of Quatre-Bras, so that Ney should not be withdrawn until free from all anxiety on that point.

While these resolutions, rather tardy and based on incomplete information, were borne to the left wing, Napoleon was making his preparations for attacking the Prussians. The corps of Count Lobau, left at first, at too great a distance towards Charleroi, was ordered to hasten to Fleurus.

The left of the *corps de bataille* under Vandamme, was drawn up fronting the village of St. Amand; the centre under Count Gérard, took up its ground facing Ligny; the guard was posted in rear of these two attacking portions; Grouchy's cavalry was deployed on the right, to keep in check the Prussian left, that had just been reinforced by the arrival of Thielmann's entire corps.

The attack commenced between two and three o'clock at St. Amand, which was at first seized by Vandamme, notwithstanding a vigorous resistance; but the Prussians, favoured by the village of La Haie, and by the heights that command it, having advanced their second line, soon retook it. Count Gérard met with similar opposition at Ligny, only a portion of which he was able to hold.

This resistance proving that the enemy mustered stronger than was supposed, Napoleon, at a quarter past three, unfortunately rather late, caused a formal order to be dispatched to Marshal Ney, ordering him to manoeuvre with his forces on Bry and St. Amand;[38] fearing

---

38. The following are the very words of this last order, which had been decisive at one o'clock, but which, it will be seen, was productive of more harm than good:

In bivouac at Fleurus,
between 3¼ and 3½ o'clock.

To Marshal Ney.

I wrote you an hour ago, that the emperor would attack the enemy in the position he has taken up, between the villages of St. Amand and Bry; at this moment the engagement is most decisive. His majesty instructs me to say, that you should at once manoeuvre in such a manner as to envelope the enemy's right, and fall with might and main on his rear; if you act with vigour this army is lost. The fate of France is in your hands; so do not hesitate in executing the movement ordered by the emperor, and move forward upon the heights of Bry and St. Amand, to concur in perhaps a decisive victory: the enemy is taken *en flagrant délit*, at the moment he seeks to join the English.   The Duke of Dalmatia

that even this order might suffer some hindrance, and knowing that d'Erlon's corps had not reached beyond Frasne, General Labédoyère was sent to communicate to this general the order given to Marshal Ney, with instructions at once to commence its execution.

While this was taking place, the engagement along the whole line continued raging. A second attack by Vandamme on St. Amand, favoured by Girard's division, that had crossed the ravine and outflanked the enemy, placed the French in possession of that village; but the brave Girard paid with his life, for a success of short duration; because Blucher, having thrown forward a portion of his reserves, the village of St. Amand was retaken and disputed with desperation.

The battle raged more furiously still at Ligny, which Gérard had frequently seized, without the power of preserving: forced to leave Hulot's division in observation on his right, and thus reduced to 10,000 combatants, he maintained his position with the most brilliant valour against more than 25,000 Prussians, in the lower portion of the village, even up to the rivulet that cuts it in two.

The guard, posted in the centre, in rear of these two attacking portions, was prepared to sustain either.

On the extreme right, Excelmans manoeuvred skilfully to prevent the left of the Prussians from debouching from Tongrenelle, while Pajol watched Boignée, and Milhaud's *cuirassiers* supported Gérard's right.

Things were in this state about half past five, and Napoleon awaited with a just impatience, to learn what was to be hoped from the movement prescribed for Ney, as the wind and the roar of a violent cannonade prevented his hearing the attack at Quatre Bras.

The emperor was preparing to bring forward his guard, when a report from General Vandamme informed him, it is said, that a strong column was visible in the direction of Wagnèle, and that Girard's division, deprived of its general and attacked at the same time by superior forces, had been forced to retire towards St. Amand-le-Hameau. General Vandamme announced, that he had at first taken this column for the detachment that Ney was to send on Marbaix; but as it was much too considerable, and as the scouts had recognized it as of the enemy, it threatened to drive him back if not promptly supported.

Though difficult to comprehend how a column could glide between Ney and Napoleon, this might, however, be a reinforcement sent to Blucher from Quatre-Bras, or probably, a corps of his own army that, having executed a movement by the ancient Roman causeway beyond Wagnèle, was in the act of turning Vandamme's left.[39] Prior to any farther action, Napoleon thought it his duty to be sure of it. The narrative from St. Helena, in exposing these facts, affirms that the emperor suspended his grand attack on this account, and sent his *aide-de-camp*, Dejean, to reconnoitre and discover who they were.[40] We are assured that this officer, at the expiration of only one hour, reported that this was Count Erlon's corps, who, instead of marching in a northerly direction towards Bry or Marbaix, had turned too much to the south, towards Villers-Peruin, attracted, undoubtedly, by the roar of two or three hundred pieces of ordnance, that thundered in the direction of St. Amand.

These assertions have been somewhat contested, and as an impartial historian, I must avow, that respecting this matter, there is nothing but doubt and confusion. As Napoleon had ordered a movement turning his left wing from the Brussels road into the direction of Bry, it was evident that this column should have been the one expected: the surprise manifested on this subject should then appear rather extraordinary.

However, if it be true that Vandamme actually took this column for the enemy's, it was at least prudent to be made certain of it, and therefore the contested mission of General Dejean would have been the most natural one; but it is necessary at least to add, that no positive order directing these troops on Bry had been given. This forgetfulness, though it might be alleged, was a manifest fault. It will be said, that Napoleon might have seen in the presence of Erlon's corps, a sufficient indication of the near arrival of Marshal Ney, to whom he undoubtedly desired to leave the task of directing his own columns: this, if admitted, does not entirely justify him; because the false direction just taken by these forces, demanded of the emperor, in every case, to state precisely what should be done to accomplish his views.

We will see farther on, the sad part played by these four fine divisions. However, about half-past six, Napoleon advanced upon Ligny with his guard, to strike the Prussians a vigorous blow, which, three hours previously, would have had more chances of success. The great confidence with which he made this splendid attack, authorizes us,

---

39. This Roman causeway, that intersects the two from Brussels and Namur, leaves the latter between Bry and Marbaix, passes half a league to the north of Wagnèle, and attains the former between Frasne and Gosselies.

40. In a letter addressed to Marshal Ney's family, General Dejean denies having had such a mission; perhaps it was confided to some other *aide-de-camp*, though this it is impossible to confirm.

moreover, in believing, that in ordering it, he firmly expected that a concurrence of a large portion of Ney's troops would not fail him, and that the column that had given Vandamme so much uneasiness was soon to cause Blucher greater anxiety.

After seven o'clock in the evening, Napoleon debouched with impetuosity through the village of Ligny with a division of the guard, seconded by Gérard's infantry, the mounted guard and Milhaud's *cuirassiers*: the enemy's centre was broken and thrown partly on Sornbref, and partly on Bry.

The Prussians fought excellently well during the whole day; but Blucher, deprived of a general reserve of cavalry, had but his infantry with which to oppose this torrent: because, seeing the guard leave the environs of St. Amand, and taking this movement as the commencement of the retreat, he had advanced with the few that yet remained on St. Amand, with the hope of pursuing the French. Very soon undeceived, he hurried back with the few cavalry he could hastily collect. But of what service is courage to a general-in-chief, in such a *mêlée*? His horse, killed by a shot, fell upon him at the instant of the disorder; the marshal remained ten minutes in the power of the French *cuirassiers* without their suspecting it, and succeeded, through the presence of mind of Nostitz, his *aide-de-camp*, in regaining Bry on a lancer's horse. It was unfortunate for some, and fortunate for others, that he was not recognized; his capture might, perhaps, have influenced the battles that followed.

Besides, this brilliant blow, struck, unfortunately, rather late, was partially arrested by the approaching night, partially by the movement which Blucher's entire left executed about Sombref, and lastly by the excellent stand made by the remains of Ziethen's and Pirch's forces between Sombref and Bry.

While the imperial troops issued so gloriously from a difficult and perilous attack, Ney proved less fortunate at Quatre-Bras. Arriving in front of this position, at two o'clock, with the three feeble divisions of Reille's corps, Piré's light cavalry division and a brigade of cuirassiers led by Kellermann, the marshal skirmished with the enemy until three o'clock, when the sound of the cannonade at St. Amand resolved him, boldly to attack the allies. But the state of things had greatly changed since the morning. General Perponcher, perceiving the great importance of Quartre-Bras, in securing the concentration of the different corps of the Anglo-Netherlanders, and afterwards in facilitating their junction with the Prussians, had taken up a position there with his own division and the brigade of the Prince of Weimar—in all, 9,000 men.

These forces, the command of which was assumed by the Prince of Orange, might have been very easily overthrown, if attacked in the morning, by two *corps d'armée*. Wellington, on reaching this spot at eleven o'clock, had ordered that the advanced posts engaged with those of Ney towards Frasne, should be recalled, so as not to be drawn into an unequal combat, previous to the arrival of reinforcements that were hurrying in from every quarter. The duke then repaired to Bry, to have an interview with Blucher, and returned between two and three o'clock. At the moment that Ney launched Reille's divisions on the enemy, Picton's English division arrived on the field of battle, and was soon followed by that under the Duke of Brunswick. Nevertheless, Ney fell upon the allies with his accustomed vigour. Foy's division, on the left, advanced on Quatre-Bras and Germioncourt, while Bachelu's attacked the village of Piermont. Prince Jerome's entered later into action, by attacking the woods of Bossut on the extreme left. The French troops vigorously pressed the enemy at all points.

Certain of the near arrival of his reinforcements, Wellington received these attacks with his usual *sang-froid*, which did not prevent the troops of the Prince of Orange and of Picton, from yielding their positions after considerable loss. The arrival of Brunswick's corps soon restored the balance; the battlefield was disputed with fury, and the Duke of Brunswick himself fell, pierced with balls, in the midst of his efforts to preserve it.

Things were in this condition, when Ney received the major-general's order, and the intelligence, that d'Erlon's corps was advancing directly on Bry. The marshal had not a single infantry soldier in reserve; he saw the masses of the enemy incessantly augmenting; nothing was left him but to charge with his *cuirassiers*, and the greater portion of them had been left with d'Erlon's, near Frasne. The marshal hastening however to the Duke de Valmy, exclaimed:

> My dear general, the safety of France is in danger; an extraordinary effort must be made; break into the English army with your cavalry; I will order Piré to support you.

Without hesitation, Kellermann at once charged at the head of this brigade of brave men, overthrew the 69th regiment, captured the batteries, and pierced through two lines up to the farm of Quatre-Bras, where the reserve of English, Hanoverian and Belgian infantry welcomed him with such a murderous fire, that his men were forced to make a large circuit in seeking to withdraw from this dangerous place. Kellermann, having had his horse killed under him, remained dismounted in the midst of the English, and with great difficulty regained his command.

Excited by this splendid charge, the French infantry renewed its efforts on Quatre-Bras and the woods of Bossut, the greater portion of which last had been occupied by Prince Jerome's division. But at this critical moment, the division of English guards and that of General Alten, coming into action after a forced march, gave Wellington such superiority, that he had nothing more to hope for. Ney had in fact sent d'Erlon imperative orders, to hasten to his succour instead of bearing on Bry: but this corps that had well nigh reached St. Amand, was too far off to arrive in time, so that the marshal was obliged to fall back on Frasne to meet him, after having lost 4,000 men *hors de combat*: the allies having entered the action successively, had lost 5,000. Wellington at first ordered a vigorous pursuit, but the retreat was protected by Roussel's division of *cuirassiers*.

In following attentively the successive train of movements that I have just pointed out, the reader will judge with what fatality d'Erlon's corps paraded uselessly along the whole line, neither reaching Bry, where it would have rendered the victory complete, nor Quatre-Bras, where it would have prevented Ney's defeat.

It will also be noticed, what strange destiny presided over all the operations of this left wing, whose inarch was by turns too slow or too hasty. If it had advanced on Quatre-Bras, on the evening of the 15th, or at least at dawn of the 16th, it would have arrived in time to crush Perponcher's division, then isolated, and to detach two divisions on Marbaix and Bry, in order to accomplish Blucher's defeat. But when, three hours later, Marshal Ney was instructed to march towards Bry himself, in order to envelop the Prussians, the thing was impossible, as he was an hour afterwards engaged at Quatre-Bras: so that it had been preferable for these two corps to have remained at Frasne, instead of pushing on so far. Much fatality and loss of time was occasioned by the faults of every one.[41]

---

41. Napoleon could have pushed as far as Fleurus on the 15th, or have taken possession of it at 6 a.m., on the 16th; he would have thus discovered Blucher's position before sending Flahaut to Marshal Ney. To obtain a complete victory on the 16th, it would have been necessary to have had the concurrence of Loban and d'Erlon's corps, and to have led but one corps of infantry and one of cavalry on Quatre-Bras. To accomplish this, the reconnoissance made by the emperor at midday, should have been made at 8 o'clock.

Before passing to the events that followed, I should here observe that though Erlon had already reached beyond Villers-Peruin, yet at the earnest recall of Ney, he marched to join him with three divisions and the light cavalry of the guard, leaving Durutte's division between Villers-Peruin and St. Amand, in case Napoleon required anew a co-operation on Bry. This division remained there all night perfectly inactive, on the flank of the rear-guard left by Blucher in this village, which it occupied until one o'clock in the morning, while Ziethen's corps retired under cover of the night on Gilly, Pirch's on Gentinne, and the left under Thielmann's orders took the direction of Gembloux.

At daybreak, Blucher's rear-guard had disappeared from Bry; Thielmann's was seen by the scouts, on the road from Sombref to Corroy le Château, towards Gembloux, intermediate between the road from Namur and that from Brussels by Wavre. Blucher, who had perhaps been wrong in accepting battle when isolated, after three o'clock, instead of then retiring beyond the Dyle by Bousseval and Cour-St.-Guibert, in order to place himself in a line with the English forces that were concentrating at Genape, felt that it was necessary promptly to repair the misfortune in the partial defeat of his army, and no longer hoping to gain Bousseval direct, resolved to rally his forces on Bulow's entire corps, which must have arrived at Gembloux during the night, and proceed by Wavre to join the English. Consequently, Thielmann was ordered to proceed to Gembloux and assemble on Bulow; the corps of Ziethen and Pirch fell back by Mont-St.-Guibert on Bierge and Aisemont.

On the 17th, the Prussian Marshal dispatched the chief of his staff to the Duke of Wellington, to concert measures for securing the junction so much desired, either in front or in rear of the forest of Soignes.

The victory just gained by the French at Ligny was a glorious one, as they had fought 60,000 men against 90,000. This success was, however, due in part to two incidents, of which the emperor was not aware: the first was, that the presence of Grouchy's cavalry on his right towards Boignée, had paralyzed Thielmann's 25,000 men posted near Tongrines and Mont-Potriaux, who were no doubt fearful of his seizing the road to Namur, thus cutting off Bulow's corps from the army, and this from its natural line of operations. The second incident was, as I have already stated, the movement of the guard, executed from St. Amand towards Ligny, at the moment when Blucher had nearly forty battalions engaged at St. Amand, causing this general to suppose that Napoleon, disheartened at not being able to force any point of his position, had commenced to beat a retreat.

With this idea, the Prussian marshal resolved to advance in person, with what remained of his reserves, in order to penetrate between St. Amand and Wagnèle, at the very instant when the imperial reserves were hurled on Ligny; so that his centre was found stripped of all support, at the moment the storm burst upon him. A *chassé croisé* was the result, bearing the main portion of the Prussian forces on St. Amand, at the decisive moment when the emperor launched his own upon Ligny, and which secured him the victory.

The French army had just obtained an advantage which, under any other circumstances, would have proved a signal one; the enemy had had, in the two battles, from eighteen to twenty thousand men killed, wounded and made prisoners; had lost forty pieces of cannon; and notwithstanding the check at Quatre-Bras, the army, full of enthusiasm and confidence, would have rushed on to new victories. They should have profited by this success, and actively pursued the enemy. Napoleon had been ignorant of Durutte's passing the night on the flank of their line of retreat, and that his advance posts might have heard, very distinctly, the uproar which such an unforeseen retreat occasioned, by the march of an immense *materiel* and the confusion of the columns; otherwise it is presumable that he would have taken measures for pressing them closer.

Yet, if the darkness contributed in arresting the pursuit that very night, it ought to have contributed also in augmenting the disorder in the retreat of the enemy's right wing, and had they acted on this occasion as the Prussians did two days after wards at Waterloo, we rest assured that the trophies would have been greater, and that the blunders committed on the two following days would have been avoided.[42] Napoleon had, during his career, given them many lessons; but they, in their turn, taught him, that a night pursuit, notwithstanding its inconveniences, might have great advantages.

On the morning of the 17th, Napoleon awaited with equal anxiety, the detailed reports of what Ney had accomplished at Quatre-Bras, and the news from Paris, where the hostile disposition of the chambers did not cause him less concern, than the revolutionary ardour of

---

42. The Prussian troops that held Bry on their right and Sombref on their left were in good order, and sufficient to arrest too bold a pursuit; nevertheless, it would have been wise to have attempted a slight attack at nightfall; no risk could be run.

the federated societies. While waiting for exact information on what was happening on the English side, he ordered Pajol's cavalry to follow the Prussians on the Namur causeway, which was their natural line of operations, at the same time that Excelmans made a reconnoissance of the road to Gembloux.

The narrative from St. Helena adds, that General Monthion was charged with the pursuit on the left, that is, in the direction of Tilly and Mont-St.-Guibert. The emperor then turned his attention to the administration, reviewed the troops and the field of battle, in order to administer to the comfort of the multitude of wounded, of both parties, with which it was strewed, and who were the more in need, as the ambulances had not been able to follow the army in its forced inarches.

To those who can recall the astonishing activity that presided over the events of Ratisbonne in 1809, of Dresden in 1813, and of Champ-Aubert and Montmirail in 1814, this time lost, will always remain inexplicable on the part of Napoleon. After a success, such as he had just achieved, it seems that, at six in the morning, he should have placed himself on the heels of the Prussians, or, as well, have fallen, with all his forces, upon Wellington, whose cavalry reserve, artillery and portion of his infantry, had only arrived that night, excessively fatigued. The necessity for not leaving his line of retreat on Charleroi to the mercy of the English general, was an imperative reason why he should have proceeded against him in preference.

It should not be supposed, that the emperor was entirely unaware of the check experienced by at Quatre-Bras; because if the marshal had not had time to make a detailed report of it, he had not surely forgotten his duty, so far as to permit him to be ignorant of the fact. This was, moreover, a greater reason for marching there without delay. However, it was well known that Ney could not obtain a great success, nor experience a great reverse, on account of the dispersed state of the Anglo-Netherland army, and of the double movement of d'Erlon's corps. Giving Wellington the morning of the 17th, in which to recover himself, was then a fault more real, perhaps, than allowing that of the 16th to Blucher. We will state further on what was the result of it. Undoubtedly the emperor had powerful motives for resigning himself to such inactivity; but these motives have never reached us.

Napoleon, having at last received, through his *aide-de-camp* Flahaut, the details of the unfortunate combat at Quatre-Bras, at the same time that Pajol reported the capture of some Prussian artillery at Mazy on the Namur road, resolved, about eleven o'clock, to march against the English with his reserve and Ney's command, while Grouchy, with his seven infantry divisions and his two cavalry corps, should vigorously pursue the Prussians. This presents one of the most serious circumstances of this campaign, and which it is my duty to expose, with all the frankness and impartiality professed by a conscientious historian.

The narrative from St. Helena affirms, that Grouchy, in receiving verbally the order to pursue the Prussians, *without losing sight of them*, received also that *of holding himself constantly between their army and the route to Brussels, which was to be taken by Napoleon*—that is to say, in such a manner that the two French masses might form between them, two interior or central lines, that could assist each other, while separating and dividing the two armies of the enemy. Marshal Grouchy, in a pamphlet for his own justification, declares, "that nothing of the kind was said to him; that on the contrary, he received, without other comment, the order to direct his pursuit on Namur and the Meuse: finally, that having indicated the desire of not withdrawing to such a distance from the main body of the army, Napoleon humorously asked him, *if he pretended to give him a lesson*." The marshal cites General Baudran, as a witness ready to attest these facts.

It would be very difficult to decide between such contradictory assertions; all that I can add is, that Major General Soult, writing on the morning of the 17th to Marshal Ney, informed him that Grouchy was to pursue the Prussians on Namur and the Meuse. Nevertheless, a little later, General Bertrand sent him a positive order to march on Gembloux. Grouchy exculpates himself equally, by reproaching the emperor for the long hours employed in reviewing the battlefield, and pending which the traces of Blucher's army were lost, and subsequently, only partially found. He also observes that the emperor, having reserved to himself the right of disposing of the troops at all points, the marshal was unable, of his own accord, to prescribe any disposition for this pursuit, and that he frequently asked for orders which were not given him.[43]

After having exposed all the facts alleged on both sides, it is my duty to observe, without any pretence to judging, that the order men-

---

43. It seems certain, that the orders given on the morning of the 17th to the different corps of cavalry for the pursuit, were addressed by the emperor direct to Pajol, Excelmans and Monthion. This last was adjutant-general, and made his reports directly to the emperor; he had reconnoitred in the direction of Tilly and Mont-St.-Guibert.

tioned in the narrative from St. Helena, was so conformable to the system of interior lines, to which Napoleon owed so great a number of his victories, that his having really given it should not be doubted; but it must also be admitted, that it would have been better, in every possible case, to have positively assigned to Grouchy, the direction intermediate between Liége and Brussels, as the one he desired his right wing to follow.

It was evident that Blucher had one of three courses to pursue, namely: to fall back on Liége, to gain Maastricht, or seek to join Wellington and resume the offensive, to avenge himself for the affront received at Ligny. The last was certainly the most skilful, the most daring, and the most conformable to the character of the Prussian general; but in order to execute it, it was necessary to renounce, somewhat, his line of retreat on the Rhine. Besides this, as Blucher had taken the road to Wavre, he could not effect the junction at all, but in rear of the forest of Soignes: because, by marching in front of it, he would be compelled to skirt its whole length, exposing his flank to the French. Napoleon must have believed, that the enemy would not dare undertake so hazardous a movement with Grouchy in close pursuit; he must have supposed, then, that if Blucher sought not to gain Maëstricht or Liége, he would march from Wavre on Brussels, a movement, that would force Wellington also to fall back on this capital or fight alone at Waterloo.

Under all these hypotheses, it was advisable to direct Grouchy on Mont-St.-Guibert and Moustier, the morning of the 17th, because the valley of the Dyle being the most favourable line for covering Napoleon's right flank, Grouchy could have crossed this river at Moustier; from thence it had been easy to draw him on to Waterloo to take part in the battle, or cause him to advance on Wavre, flanked towards St. Lambert, by Excelmans' dragoons and an infantry division. By this means, the emperor would have been certain of his power to collect all his right wing about him, if Wellington accepted battle on the 18th in front of the forest of Soignes, and could have counted on the impossibility of the Prussians' co-operating.

Be that as it may, the two fractions of the imperial army should have moved at the same time, in proceeding to their respective destinations. The reserve, led by Napoleon, left however first, to join Ney and the left wing at Quatre-Bras, in order to attack the English if they stood their ground; his advanced guard moved at ten o'clock; the guard following at eleven. The right wing moved later still; Vandamme, who formed the advance, proceeded at first to Point-du-Jour (an inn situated at the fork of the roads to Gembloux and Namur); Gérard's corps did not leave Sombref till after three o'clock. Marshal Grouchy, having received orders to inarch on Gembloux, of which we have spoken above, and the intelligence that General Excelmans was in presence of the Prussians near this city, hastened there in person, directing Vandamme and Gérard on the same point. Pajol alone patrolled with his hussars and Teste's division, in the direction of Mazy and Temploux. We leave them there, in order to follow the operations of the imperial army.

Napoleon, on arriving near Genape, met the English rear-guard. The weather was frightful, the windows of heaven seemed to be opened, and yet the troops did not the less exhibit an extreme ardour in the pursuit of the enemy. The Duke of Wellington did not hear, until eight o'clock on the morning of the 17th, and that by accident, of Blucher's defeat (the officer who was bearer of the news losing his way in the dark, had been killed). We can judge what would have been his embarrassment, had Napoleon marched against him at daybreak. The English general hastened to place his *impedimenta* in retreat, while his exhausted cavalry took some repose.

At ten o'clock, his columns were in march on the Brussels' causeway, protected by all the cavalry concentrated under the orders of Lord Uxbridge, who took position at Genape behind the Dyle, to allow the army time to gain ground. This general officer displayed, on this occasion, the same *aplomb* of which he had given proof in Spain,[44] by charging with his English guards, those who were rash enough to dare attempt the passage of the defile in his presence. The French followed him, step by step, as far as Maison du Roi, on the heights of Planchenois. where the army arrived at nightfall.

The enemy manifested his intention to maintain the position in front of the forest of Soignes. At first, it was thought, that this was but a strong rear-guard covering the march of columns through the forest; it was very soon perceived that the entire army was present; but as it was too late in the day to commence an action, the different corps bivouacked near Planchenois. The rain continued to fall in torrents till the next morning.

At three o'clock in the morning, Napoleon went the rounds of the posts, and assured himself that the army had not stirred; Wellington

---

44. Lord Uxbridge is the same personage, who rendered himself so illustrious in Spain under the name of Sir Arthur Paget, and who now bears the title of Marquis d'Anglesey. He distinguished himself at Benevento, and in many other *rencontres*.

had then decided on accepting battle; he was delighted, regarding it as a stroke of fortune that the two hostile armies thus appeared in the lists, isolated, each in its turn.

Meanwhile, to profit by this happy chance with security, it behooved him to be assured, that no junction of the two armies could however take place. To this effect, it is affirmed that Napoleon had, about dusk, sent a courier to Grouchy with orders to occupy the defile of St. Lambert immediately, so that, if he took no active part in the fête by falling on the English left, he could at least cover the right flank and give them some uneasiness.

This order, the existence of which has been denied, was addressed to Wavre, under the conviction that the marshal had reached this city during the 17th, having but seven or eight leagues to pass over from Sombref.[45] About midnight, the emperor received this marshal's report, stating that he had reached Gembloux at five in the afternoon, and would spend the night there, although he had travelled but two leagues; from this it was evident that he would not receive the order directed to Wavre. If we would credit the same narrative, the confirmation was forwarded by the Gembloux road, hoping that he would receive it in time.

The rain, bad roads, and forced marches had worn out the French army. Napoleon might have found it somewhat to his interest, to have given it repose, and then to have dislodged Wellington by manoeuvring, but 300,000 of the enemy were on their way to invade la Lorraine, and required the chief of state with his principal forces on the Moselle; on the other hand, Blucher would soon rally and be reinforced, and thus everything demanded that he should finish with the

---

45. Some persons have been astonished at Napoleon's supposition, that Grouchy had, on the 17th, already readied Wavre, as they had only separated towards midday, and two hours were necessary for the troops, altogether unprepared, to set out on the march. There is something for and against, in these statements; Napoleon, departing from Ligny, pushed on as far as La Belle Alliance; now, Grouchy, having but one league more to pass over to gain Wavre, could, strictly speaking, very well have accomplished it. What should be a matter of astonishment is, that of supposing Grouchy at Wavre, if he had at first been directed on Namur, as the major-general's correspondence would make us believe; then afterwards on Gembloux, as General Bertrand's letter proves. Be that as it may, the order cited is not found among the records of the staff; and besides, it did not reach its destination, the officer having fallen at night in the midst of the Prussian posts and been killed As to the confirmation of this order, no trace of it has been found, unless the question in point be a letter of the major-general, written at 10 a. m., to Gros-Caillou, and which Grouchy received at four in the afternoon, in front of Wavre.

English as soon as possible.

The emperor had reconnoitred their position; they occupied, in front of Mont-St.-Jean, a beautiful plateau, the slope of whose sides was favourable for firing, and from which all the movements of the French could be discovered. The right extended to the rear of Braine la Leud, and a corps of Netherlander of 15,000 men were besides detached as far as Hall, to cover the causeway from Mons to Brussels. The position in itself had great defensive advantages, because the villages of Braine and de Merbes, the *château* of Hougomont, la Haie Sainte, la Haie and Frischermont formed so many advanced bastions, that prevented any approach to the line; but it rested back against the vast forest of Soignes: now Napoleon thought, that if it be an advantage for a rear-guard to be thus posted, considering that the defile protects its retreat, it is not so for a large army with its immense *materiel* and its numerous cavalry, having as communications but a narrow causeway and two crossroads, encumbered with parks, the wounded, etc. etc.[46] He therefore believed that all the chances were in his favour.

The opportunity of giving battle being acknowledged, it remained to decide what system would be most expedient for attacking the English. To manoeuvre by the left, in order to overthrow their right, was a difficult matter, and led to nothing decisive; this was not a good strategic direction, as it would be entirely removed from the centre of operations, which was naturally connected by the right, with Grouchy, and with the road to Lorraine: besides this, the enemy's right wing was protected by the farm of Hougomont, and by the two large boroughs of Braine la Leud and Merbe-Braine.

To attack with the right, in order to crush the English left, was much more preferable, as this would maintain a direct relation, or an interior line with Grouchy, and would prevent the junction of the two hostile armies: but to gain, *en masse*, this extreme left, it would be necessary to extend beyond Frischermont, leaving open the line of retreat, and venturing into the obstructed country of St. Lambert, where a defeat had been without remedy.

It remained for Napoleon to take a middle course, that of renewing the manoeuvre executed at Wagram and Moscowa, (Borodino,) that is, to assail the left at the same time that he drove in the centre. It was the best plan of battle he could have adopted, and with him, it

---

46. This is one of the gravest questions of the grand tactics of battles. General Jomini has discussed it in his last *Precis de l'Art de la Guerre*, and inclines to Wellington's opinion in opposition to Napoleon's.

had often proved successful. To force the centre only is difficult and dangerous, unless it happens to be a weak and unfurnished point, as at Austerlitz, Rivoli, and Montenotte; but we do not always find an enemy sufficiently complaisant, as to allow us such an advantage, and it would be absurd to expect it from an army following a good system, or, rather, that understands the principles of war. But to make an attack upon a wing, overthrow it, and at the same time fall upon the point, where this wing joins the centre, with a large force, is an operation always advantageous when well executed.

Napoleon resolved, then, to attempt it. However, instead of concentrating the bulk of his masses against the left, as at Borodino, he directed them on the centre; the extreme left was not to be assailed, but by the division forming the right of Erlon's corps, which would attack Papelotte and la Haie; Ney was to lead the three other divisions on the right of la Haie Sainte;[47] Reille's corps would support this movement on the left of the Mont-St.-Jean causeway; Bachelu's and Foy's divisions, between this causeway and the farm of Hougomont; Jerome's, led in fact by Guilleminot, was to attack this farm, the salient point of the enemy's line, the *château* and park wall of which, Wellington had crenelled, and where he had posted the English guards. Count Lobau, with the 6th corps and a mass of cavalry, would follow the centre in a third and fourth line, on the right and left of the causeway, to support Ney's attack on la Haie Sainte: lastly, twenty-four battalions of guards and de Valmy's *cuirassiers*, were to second the decisive shock, wherever needed, in a fifth and sixth line.

Such was the plan that many incidents deranged, and which Napoleon can leave, without fear, to the scrutiny of the masters of the art. It could not be bettered, unless moving his reserves a little nearer his right, thus giving more vigour to the effort between Papelotte and the Charleroi causeway. It would have signified much for the success of this project, had a sudden attack been made in the morning, but torrents of rain had fallen all night; the weather was beginning to clear; it required some hours to give a little consistency to the soft ground, and this time was employed in forming the army in position.[48]

---

47. It is necessary not to confound la Haie Sainte, on the centre, with la Haie on the left wing of the allies.

48. We cannot share this opinion, which has been set forth by Napoleon, in Book 9 from St. Helena; when, even had a splendid sun succeeded the rain, four hours would not have sufficed to dry such a ground; besides, this sun did not appear; misty weather followed the storm; nothing then prevented him from making the new effort at 9 a. m.; it could have been done as well as at one, (continued next page.)

The cannonade and musketry commenced, at 11 o'clock, against the farm of Hougomont, which Jerome sought to carry; it pleased the emperor to open the battle at this point. A few moments after, Ney's light cavalry appeared towards Frischermont, at the opposite extremity, where were exchanged a few cannon shot. It was then found that the rivulet, though narrow and slightly embanked, was very miry, and that it would be necessary to turn it by the west of Smouhen, as it would prove troublesome to cross it lower down, in face of the enemy's batteries. Compelled thus to turn a portion of his right upon their centre, Ney succeeded finally in forming his four divisions of d'Erlon's corps, and his artillery only succeeded, after incredible efforts, in taking position in the muddy ground, with their pieces sunk to the naves of their wheels.

The marshal immediately opened a heavy fire upon the enemy's left, and only waited for the signal, to burst upon it. Napoleon was about giving it, after midday, when rather strong columns were discovered on the right in the direction of Lasne and St. Lambert; this might be the enemy, or the detachment demanded of Grouchy. The emperor immediately pushed forward 3,000 horse under General d'Homond towards Pajeau, at once to reconnoitre the state of things; cover the flank, if needed, were it the enemy, or effect a junction with Grouchy, if he it was who had arrived.[49] It behooved him to undertake nothing, before receiving a report of this reconnoissance. Very shortly afterwards, a Prussian hussar was brought with an intercepted letter; he announced the approach of Bulow's corps, which he estimated at 30,000 men.

Notwithstanding this serious *contre-temps*, nothing seemed desperate. Under all other circumstances, it had perhaps been better to have deferred the battle; but what could be done?—shot had been exchanged; it was necessary to continue the fight, or shamefully decamp before Wellington, with whom Napoleon measured himself for the first time. Apart from the point of honour, what moral effect would

---

and the Prussians would have arrived after the blow had been struck. In the then state of affairs, this delay of four hours was a blunder; but the arrival of Blucher was not expected, and the troops required rest.

49. It was hard to believe that this was Grouchy, after the reports received from him during the night. However, had he taken, on the morning of the 18th, the road to Moustier instead of that to Wavre, by Sart à Valain, the case was not an impossible one. Besides, this column discovered about twelve, was only Bulow's advance guard; the corps did not arrive till four, on account of a violent conflagration that had prevented it from defiling through Wavre.

this retreat produce, if he fled without unsheathing his sword against the English? What could he hope for his cause, when the Russians, Austrians and the whole Germanic empire, should burst upon Lorraine, the Austro-Sardinians upon Dauphiny, the Swiss upon Franche-Comté, and the Spaniards upon Languedoc? If Bulow came with a score of thousands, the belief should be that he was closely followed by Grouchy, and in that case, the arrival of this new enemy would not change the chances of the battle.

The emperor then ordered Ney to commence the attack, and in order to secure the threatened flank, he moved Count Lobau's two divisions, *en potence*, towards Planchenois, where they could, if needed, serve as reserves to Ney, or otherwise, in a measure, oppose Bulow. If this latter was closely pursued by Grouchy, the Prussian corps would thus find itself between two fires, in a cut-throat position, and would become an additional trophy for the conqueror.

Nearly one hundred pieces of ordnance open upon the enemy's centre, to the right and left of la Haie Sainte; it is there that the great effort is to be made, and if Ney, seconded by Lobau and the guard, succeeds in penetrating here, as he did at Friedland, they will seize on the point where the causeway enters the forest of Soignes, which is the sole retreat for the enemy. But Count Lobau's support is soon to fail him in this vigorous effort, and render success doubtful.

About one o'clock, Ney marched forward at the head of d'Erlon's corps, which was formed of the divisions in separate columns, so as to cross with more rapidity the space that separated it from the enemy.[50] This movement, executed in very deep columns, closed in mass, under a murderous fire, and through a terrible mud, was accomplished without much wavering; a portion of his artillery remained in rear, and continued to counter-batter that of the enemy from a distance, while the infantry effected the passage of the ravine. Though the formation in columns had left between the divisions very considerable intervals, they were not, however, sufficiently great for deploying them.

The different narratives heretofore published, differ materially as to the manner in which this first attack was executed: some have it, that the four divisions of d'Erlon's corps, thus formed into as many masses,

---

50. It appears that each division formed a single mass of eight or ten battalions, marching in rear of each other. It is uncertain, whether all these battalions were formed in columns of attack, or deployed into eight or ten lines, but they formed a very deep mass. It also appears that Marcognet's division made a flank movement to draw nearer the centre, and that the English took advantage of its waverings.

in echelon, the left in front, were directed against the position of the allies' left wing, slighting the post of la Haie-Sainte, which was left behind them. Others have the 2nd division of d'Erlon's corps marching on this post, and the 4th on that of Smouhen, nearly simultaneous with the attack of the position.

Nevertheless, I have every reason to believe, that, in fact, these divisions, in deep columns, moved together to attack the position, the front line of which was composed of General Perponcher's Belgians, on the right of the Mont-St.-Jean causeway, while Durutte's division advanced on Smouhen, or at least in conjunction with Jaquinot's light cavalry, kept in check the enemy's extreme left.[51]

Braving all the difficulties, which the soft ground offered to the movements of masses thus agglomerated, together with the fire of a formidable artillery, the 1st and 3rd divisions reach the front line of the enemy at the point held by General Bylandt's Belgian brigade, (Perponcher's division,) which they drive in after a vigorous onset. But, far from having accomplished their task, they are suddenly assailed by Picton's English division, posted in a second line, and lying behind a ridge that favours them. Here a furious combat takes place; the English infantry deployed in line, envelop with its concentrated fire the head and flank of this heavy mass, which can oppose but a few musket shots, more calculated to diminish its enthusiasm than cause the enemy any loss. General Picton falls dead; but his troops stand firm, and the French column, arrested by their murderous fire, turns and gives way.

At this moment, Lord Uxbridge lets loose General Ponsonby's English cavalry, to charge them in flank and spread the disorder: emboldened by this success, the English squadrons throw themselves into the interval between the 2nd and 3rd columns, where they gain the

---

51. Great confusion reigns in all the narratives, published up to this time, on the battle of Waterloo. Some have the left of the position attacked by the four divisions farthest off; others say that Durutte's advanced on Smouhen, and Quiot's on la Haie Sainte. The *Victoires et Conquetes* speak of a grand column formed of the 2nd and 3rd divisions, (Donzeiot's and Marcognet's). This would then be Quiot's—the first that must have attacked la Haie Sainte. Nevertheless, German authors have as many columns as divisions; they speak of a brigade of *cuirassiers*, Valmy's or Milhaud's, seconding this first attack, and French narrators say not a word about it. They state that the eagles of the 45th and 105th regiments were captured in the grand column; but, one of these regiments belonged to the 1st division and the other to the 3rd. Lastly, other versions would make us believe, that Durutte did not advance on Smouhen till 4 p. m. It is impossible to make out anything from such a chaos.

same advantage; finally, carried away by their ardour, these squadrons rush on Ney's reserve artillery, a portion of which remained in rear on account of the mire; they sabre the soldiers of the train and the cannoniers, lead away the horses, and thus deprive the infantry of part of its ordnance. Napoleon launches Milhaud's *cuirassiers*, supported by a brigade of lancers, against these reckless fellows; in a few moments this cavalry of the enemy is destroyed, and Ponsonby killed; but the French infantry has been shaken and a portion of the artillery rendered immovable. Meanwhile, Ney has ordered the attack of the farm of la Haie-Sainte by a brigade of d'Erlon's corps, which at first experiences an active resistance and serious loss.

While these things were taking place against the left of the allies, and on the point where this wing joined the centre, Jerome Bonaparte, seconded by Foy, had with difficulty dislodged the enemy from the park of Hougomont; but all efforts proved fruitless against the *château* and the crenellated farm, where Wellington himself led reinforcements to the English guards, who defended this important post with admirable valour.

The Duke of Wellington, certain of the near arrival of Blucher's entire army, and too happy at having gained half the day by the delay of the attack, had determined to conquer or to die. Seeing that all efforts were directed against his centre and left, he hastened to shorten his line, by withdrawing from Braine-la-Leud and Merbes twenty battalions of Belgians and Brunswickers, which he placed successively in reserve, in rear of the right and centre. Then, he in person, conducted reinforcements to the English guards, now at the point of succumbing at Hougomont, and reanimated their ardour.

General Foy, on his side, wishing to second the attacks which Jerome's division (led by General Guilleminot) was making on the *château*, sought to pass this post and fall upon Lord Hill's line and the Brunswickers, formed behind an excavated road that ran along a great portion of the enemy's front, from the *château* of Nivelle to the vicinity of Papelotte. But struck by a ball in the shoulder, and seeing his troops mowed down by a murderous fire, without hope of dislodging the enemy, Foy had to give up this design; the combat at this point degenerated to a cannonade and a scattering fire, without reciprocal advantages.

During this interval, Ney had put to the test all his energy and presence of mind, in recovering from the checks received in his first attacks; his right in possession of Smouhen, debouched on Papelotte, and the marshal himself led a second assault on la Haie Sainte. Donzelot's division, supported on the left of the causeway by a brigade of the Duke de Valmy's *cuirassiers*, and on the right by a brigade of General Quiot's infantry, succeeded finally in expelling the Scotch and Hanoverian battalions from it: at four o'clock these troops were masters of these two points, after efforts the most glorious.

Pending this struggle, the emperor passed down Ney's line and that of Milhaud's cavalry, through a storm of bullets; General Devaux, commanding the artillery of the guard and reserve, was killed at his side; a sad loss, at a moment when he was to be called upon, to renew the splendid manoeuvre of Wagram.

The simultaneous capture of la Hale Sainte and Papelotte, about four o'clock, still continued all the chances in favour of the assailants. But at the time that Wellington was accumulating his forces on the centre, Napoleon was compelled to withdraw his own, because of the information that Bulow was at last debouching from the woods of Frischermont on Planchenois. If we would wish to follow exactly the chronological order of the enemy's movements, we would have to recall here the doings of the Prussian army since the previous evening, but it seems more advisable to narrate the events, in the same order in which they came to Napoleon's knowledge. We will then return, farther on, to Blucher's operations, limiting ourselves to pointing out, here, the successive arrivals of his corps.

At the moment of Ney's success in carrying la Haie Sainte, Bulow, having debouched from the woods of Frischermont, attacked the Count de Lobau, and, thanks to his superiority, drove him on Planchenois, by overthrowing his right. Napoleon then learned with certainty, that Grouchy was not following this Prussian column; it was no longer possible to labour under the slightest illusion; all that could be done war, to dispute the honour of this fatal battlefield, in which his line was out-flanked to such an extent, that the Prussian bullets nearly reached the Charleroi causeway in rear of his centre.

Success was not at all possible, but by dint of perseverance he might force the enemy to retreat. He resolved then, about five o'clock, to get rid of Bulow by a vigorous *coup de main*, in directing against him the young guard, under the brave Duhesme, supported by General Morand with a portion of the old guard, then immediately to attempt a last effort against Wellington, with his entire reserves. While awaiting the issue of this manoeuvre, Ney should have been satisfied with holding la Haie Sainte and Papelotte.

Meanwhile, the marshal, finding himself isolated by the direction of the attacks of Reille's corps, about the *château* of Hougomont, earnestly asked for reinforcements. For want of infantry the emperor assigned him Milhaud's *cuirassiers*. Wellington, on his part, encouraged by Bulow's attack, and strengthened by the troops from his extreme right, had conceived the hope of again taking possession of the park of Hougomont and the farm of la Haie Sainte. With this object, he had, at five o'clock, launched the Hanoverians, on this last post, simultaneously with Lord Hill's English on the first. At this very instant, Ney, whose troops suffered terribly from the enemy's fire, seeing the light cavalry of his right driven back by that of the English, sought to seize, at all hazards, the plateau of Mont-St.-Jean, by casting his brave *cuirassiers* upon the centre of the allies.

Unfortunately, his infantry was so shaken, that it could offer but feeble succour. However, these squadrons meeting the Hanoverians marching on la Haie Sainte, fell upon them, sabring one regiment, carrying off the artillery posted on the enemy's front, breaking a square of the German legion, but attempting the same upon others without success; the enemy formed in squares by regiments, sheltered the cannoniers and artillery horses, and by a well sustained fire baffled the efforts of this heroic cavalry,[52] which, charged in its turn by Lord Somerset's English cavalry, was forced to rally, and effected it with audacity under the very fire of the enemy's line.

Undoubtedly, it had been preferable had this charge been executed a little earlier, in conjunction with d'Erlon's first attack, or had been deferred until the return of the young guard from extricating Count Lobau, so as to make a combined effort of the three arms reunited. But the plateau was crowned, it was necessary to sustain what was already accomplished, or look upon the loss of Ney's troops. Napoleon then, after six o'clock, orders Kellermann (Valmy) to advance with his *cuirassiers* on the left of la Haie Sainte causeway, and overthrow everything in his path; the heavy cavalry of the guard follow this movement, and engage the enemy, it is said, contrary to the emperor's intentions.[53]

At the sight of all these reinforcements, Milhaud also renews his attacks. These 10,000 horse make terrible havoc in the enemy's line, car-

---

52. The Duke of Wellington himself assured me, at the Congress of Verona, that he had never seen anything more admirable in war, than the ten or twelve reiterated charges of the French *cuirassiers* upon the troops of all arms.
53. Napoleon might have intended to preserve this precious nucleus in reserve, but assuredly he had placed it at Ney's disposal.

rying off sixty pieces of cannon from the front of their position, and breaking two squares; but the rest of the English infantry oppose an admirable front; the fire of the 2nd line, destroys the French squadrons that have become scattered in their charges; lastly, the English, Belgian, Hanoverian and Brunswickerian cavalry, led by Lord Uxbridge, form in fine order to charge in their turn, success cannot fail them. To remain in such a situation is impossible; it is then necessary to sound the rally at some distance, abandon the captured artillery, in fact give the English cannoniers the liberty of returning to their guns and crush anew this body of cavalry.

It nevertheless turns about and drives back Lord Uxbridge's squadrons upon their infantry.[54] It would be necessary to borrow the most poetic forms and expressions of an epic, to depict with any truthfulness the glorious efforts of this cavalry, and the impassive perseverance of its adversaries. We can besides judge, what would have been the result of these brilliant charges, had Lobau's corps and the young guard been able to follow the *cuirassiers* in their course, instead of being engaged towards Planchenois, making head against the Prussians. Eyewitnesses have attested to the disorder that was apparent among a portion of the allied troops, and to the alarm that spread as far as Brussels, where the French were momentarily expected.

Napoleon had greater hopes of obtaining the victory, as, in the interval, Bulow, attacked by Lobau and Dushesme, supported by a detachment of the old guard, under General Morand, had just been driven on to the Pajeau road, and the booming of Grouchy's cannon being heard on the Dyle, it could be supposed that he would at least hold in check the surplus of Blucher's army. Undoubtedly this victory had not led to immense results, but it was already more than won: to decide it finally, the emperor, at half-past seven o'clock, ordered the entire guard to be concentrated, in order to carry the position of Mont-St.-Jean.

The illusion was not of long duration; the French cavalry had scarcely rallied its victorious squadrons, when new hostile columns from Ohain, were discovered from the plateau: this was Blucher himself, who arrived with Ziethen's corps in the direction of Papelotte. At the same time, Pirch's corps having debouched from Lasne, had already come into action, to second Bulow at Planchenois.

Though difficult for Napoleon to estimate the strength of all these

---

54. Lord Uxbridge (Marquis d'Anglesey,) had his leg taken off by a shot; I am uncertain whether it happened at the instant of this attack, or later.

forces, they were more than sufficient to snatch victory from him. It is said, however, that he flattered himself with leading fortune under his banner, by refusing his right threatened by very strong forces, in order to bring all his efforts to bear through his left on Hougomont and Mont-St.-Jean; a rash change of front, that necessarily abandoned the line of retreat to Charleroi, to follow a new one on the Nivelle causeway, and which, moreover, destroyed all communication with Grouchy. Had the success of this measure been in the least problematical, its execution had become impossible; even the assembling of the entire guard could not be effected: disorder began to infect the cavalry, and Durutte's division, menaced by three times their number on the plateau, between Smouhen and the causeway; it was necessary to fly to d'Erlon's support, without even waiting for the return of the guard commanded by Morand, as well as other detachments.

Napoleon placed himself at the head of Friant's division, the only disposable body, and conducted it to la Haie Sainte, at the same time that he ordered Reille to make dispositions for another attack on Hougomont. This reinforcement, led by Napoleon, gave courage to the French cavalry, and to the *débris* of d'Erlon's corps; if Morand's entire division had been there, an attack might have been made with some chances of success; but forced to hold some battalions in hand towards la Belle Alliance, Napoleon was unable to assemble but four, on the summit of the plateau in front of la Haie Sainte. Ney, sword in hand, led them against the enemy.

Meanwhile, Wellington, certain of the near arrival of Blucher on his left, thought of retaking the park of Hougomont and la Haie Sainte; he had drawn Brunswick's division and a Belgian brigade on the latter point, at the moment when this handful of the brave guard proceeded to attack, with levelled bayonets, the broken line of the Anglo-Hanoverians.

Aware of the importance of this movement, the Prince of Orange quickly throws himself before them at the head of a Nassau regiment, while Brunswick's division attacks them from another quarter; but the Prince falls, wounded by a shot, while pointing out to them the road to victory. The brave soldiers of the old guard, at first repel the shock, but, deprived of support, in the midst of the enemy, which is being reinforced by a Belgian brigade *de chasse*, surrounded by a sheet of fire that consumes them, they feel the moment is at hand when their cause will be lost forever, and with difficulty retire to the foot of the plateau, that had cost so much blood. Napoleon having, meanwhile, reassembled the six other battalions of the old guard, that had been detached on different points, is in the act of seconding these efforts on Mont-St.-Jean, when the disorder which begins to be manifest on the right of d'Erlon's corps, forces him to form these battalions into squares, on the right of la Haie Sainte.

While these things are passing on the front of the French army, between eight and nine o'clock, the young guard and Lobau struggle with rare bravery against the constantly increasing forces of the Prussians. Strengthened by the arrival of Pirch's corps, Bulow finishes the overwhelming of the remainder of these *braves*, whose distress is redoubled by the departure of the old guard, and by the entrance into action of Blucher and Ziethen on their left flank. On the arrival of this last, the cavalry of Wellington's left wing, (Vivian's and Vandeleur's brigades,) that had suffered least of all, gallop to the centre to his support. Ziethen, who, at eight o'clock, had debouched at the vertex of the angle formed by the French line towards Frischermont, easily overthrows Durutte, at the same time that he out-flanks the left of the crotchet formed by Lobau and the young guard. Pirch turns Planchenois, which Bulow attacks in front.

All this portion of the imperial army, crushed, overrun and surrounded by quadruple numbers, crowd upon each other and seek safety in flight. Duhesme and Barrois are severely wounded; Lobau, in endeavouring to rally his men, falls into the hands of the enemy; Pelet shows front with a handful of heroes, about whom crowd a scattered few. The very report of General Gnisenau on this celebrated battle, will ever remain the most splendid testimony to the heroic defence of these twelve or fifteen thousand French against sixty thousand Prussians, favoured, moreover, by the nature of the battlefield, which, rising on their side into an amphitheatre, gave to their numerous artillery a terrible ascendency over that of their adversaries.

Judging from the continuance of the fire, that Blucher and Bulow were giving the finishing stroke, Wellington on his part assembles all the best troops possible, retakes the park of Hougomont, and about nine o'clock bursts on the old guard with an overwhelming superiority, at the same time that Blucher's Prussian cavalry outflanks Durutte, and thus gets in rear of the line. A furious combat takes places; Generals Friant and Michel are seriously wounded; all that remain of the cuirassiers and cavalry of the guard perform wonders; but their position is no longer tenable. Assailed by sixty thousand Prussians concentrated on Wellington's left, the whole French right flows back, in the greatest disorder, on la Belle Alliance; the guard that shows front to the English is also forced to give way; Wellington's cavalry profits by the disorder, and introduces itself between Reille's corps and the guard, formed into different squares, at the same time that Blucher takes the line in reverse. These masses of cavalry, render the rallying of d'Erlon's and Reille's corps impossible.

For a long time the Prussian artillery ploughs with its shot the Charleroi causeway, quite far in rear of the line, and contributes not a little in redoubling the disorder, which night, in spreading her wings, succeeds in completing. The infantry, cavalry and artillery take, pell-mell, the road to Genape, and some even endeavour to gain the Neville route, being less molested than that to Charleroi.

Dragged far from the last gallant few, who, under Cambronne, show front to the enemy, Napoleon finds himself separated from them, and reduced to the alternative of regaining the Genape route across the country, accompanied by his staff, having no longer in hand even a single battalion, at the head of which he might seek death in the ranks of the foe. Wellington, who with impetuosity has changed from the defensive to the offensive, meets Blucher at la Belle Alliance, (the name of a farm, to which the events gave a whimsical pertinency). This meeting, which many have wished to attribute to chance, had been skilfully planned; it is time to say by what concurrent circumstances it was effected.

We left Grouchy departing for Gembloux, at noon of the 17th. We remember that Thielmann's corps had withdrawn from Sombref in this very direction, undoubtedly, in order to rally on Bulow, who had just arrived after a forced march of twelve leagues, while the right of Blucher's army, composed of Ziethen's and Pirch's corps, retired by Mont-St.-Guibert on Bierge and Aisemont. Be that as it may, Grouchy reached Gembloux, and was informed during the evening that Bulow and Thielmann had reunited there in the morning, and had then taken the direction of Wavre. These two corps formed a mass of 52,000 men.

Gérard's corps not arriving at Gembloux till eleven o'clock at night, in consequence of a violent storm that had destroyed the roads and jaded his troops, Grouchy resolved to advance on Wavre the next morning at six, with Vandamme's corps, Gérard to follow alone at eight o'clock. This resolution, howsoever much it seemed in conformity with the orders Napoleon had given him, to follow on the heels of the Prussians, was an actual blunder. In fact, from the time that

Blucher relinquished the natural base of the Meuse, it was evident that he thought only of uniting with Wellington, retaking the offensive and revenge himself for the affront he had just received: from that moment, even admitting that Napoleon had at first indicated the pursuit on Namur, Grouchy being aware that this order could not possibly be executed, became again master of his actions, according to his own inspirations; moreover, the order transmitted afterwards, through General Bertrand, to proceed on Gembloux, had sufficiently indicated the end the marshal was to attain. To pursue the Prussians was his duty, but he had many ways of performing it. One consisted in merely following the trail of the retreating columns, the other in alone harassing the rear-guard by means of light bodies, directing his principal forces on the flanks of the columns, to attack them in earnest, as the Russians did in 1812 at Wiasma, Krasnoe, and at the Bérésina.[55]

Under the circumstances in which Grouchy was placed, it was more than ever his duty to follow this plan; because his first mission was to prevent the Prussians from turning back against Napoleon, and the second point alone was to harass him in his retreat. Now, by marching along the Prussian columns with his infantry, while his light cavalry harassed his rear, he would have had the double advantage of opposing all attempts at a junction with the English, and avoiding the battle in the defile, which otherwise he would be constrained to give at Wavre. Three principal roads were open to him: that on the right by Sart à Valain, which had been followed by Bulow; that on the left by Mont-St. Guibert, from whence he could advance on Wavre, either by following the right bank of the Dyle, or crossing this river at Moustier, and reaching Wavre by the left bank, thus avoiding a horrible combat in a defile. All were equally long, but that on the left approached within two leagues of Napoleon's army, and on the contrary, that on the right deviated as much farther from it. Nearly a day's march was gained by the first, without considering that he interposed between the two allied armies.

The marshal should not, then, have hesitated; he should at daybreak, on the 18th, have marched with all speed on Moustier, with Excelmans, Vandamme and Gérard, directing Pajol's cavalry and Teste's division on Wavre, in pursuit of the enemy's rear-guard.[56] Being able,

---
55. See what General Jomini says on the subject of lateral pursuits, in his last *Precis de l'Art de la Guerre* 2 vol.; published by Anselin.
56. This strategic movement would have been one of those, that build up the reputation of a great captain. It is probable that (continued next page.)

to reach Moustier by ten o'clock, he could have then forwarded his infantry on Wavre by Limale, pushing Excelmans' dragoons on St. Lambert, or else have marched to Lasne himself, from which place he would have heard, at noon, the violent cannonade at Waterloo.

Instead of taking this wise resolution, Grouchy, undoubtedly desirous of following to the letter, on the heels of the Prussians as ordered, and deceived by reports that still signalled Prussian columns in the direction of Pervez, directed his own on Sart à Valain, this being the route Bulow had taken. The marshal decided thus, the more so as he was perfectly ignorant that half the Prussian army had passed by Gentines and Mont-St. Guibert, the reconnoissance made in this direction on the 17th, having been reported to Napoleon and not to him. To this fault, that of starting at too late an hour, can be added; and as a consequence, towards noon only Vandamme had got beyond Sart à Valain, and the head of Gérard's column had but reached this village.

Grouchy had just been rejoined by this general, when the sound of a cannonade, hollow and distant, but lively and well sustained, announced an important battle: Count Gérard then proposed to the marshal, to take that direction immediately, persuaded that in marching *au canon*, as Ney did at Eylau, he might decide the victory.[57]

However wise this advice might have been in itself, we must avow that the same advantages would not have accrued, as if this movement had been operated from Gembloux at daybreak, and that his arrival would have been too late to prove decisive; because, supposing that Vandamme, whose corps was in advance, could commence moving at one o'clock, and this on the heights of St. Martin, it is probable he would not have reached Moustier before four. Now the frightful state of the roads, the bad condition of the bridges, the boggy defiles of the Dyle, and above all, the presence of Thielmann's corps, which extended from the heights of Bierge to Limale, opposing his crossing, authorize us in believing, that Grouchy would not have reached Lasne or St. Lambert before seven or eight in the evening. Then, Thielmann's and Pirch's corps, formed in rear of the rivulet of Lasne, preventing

---

Napoleon, placed at Gembloux, in Grouchy's situation, would have executed it; however, he made no mention of it, and prescribed nothing of the kind; he even approved the movement on Wavre: the fact is, he never believed in the daring flank movement executed by Blucher.

57. The maxim to march *au canon* is generally a very wise one, as it is at bottom but a concentric manoeuvre, the effect of which is nearly always certain; under particular circumstances, there are exceptions; the Battle of Bautzen is one of the most striking examples of it.

him from pushing on farther, Bulow and Ziethen would not the less have decided the battle of Waterloo; it certainly would have proved less disastrous, for the conquered, but there was not the slightest possibility of gaining it.

Great controversy has arisen on this point; each one has interpreted in his own way and according to his own views, the results that would have followed this movement advised by Gérard. To judge properly of the consequences that might have been expected from it, it must not be forgotten, that Thielmann's corps, posted on the heights of Bierge, with information as far as Limale, had orders to follow that of Pirch on St. Lambert, in case Grouchy did not make his appearance towards Wavre, and that one of his divisions had already marched to this effect. If it be true that Grouchy's troops, taking at noon the Nil-St. Martin route on Moustier, would have arrived there between three and four o'clock, they would certainly have been immediately engaged with Thielmann's 20,000 men, forcibly suspending, and perhaps stopping his march.

If they had wished to debouch by Limale, this force of the enemy would have been met earlier. On the other hand, Pirch's columns, that at this moment were advancing on Lasne, would have probably halted, seeing themselves thus menaced in reverse; even admitting that they had retrograded in order to support Thielmann; but then Bulow had already concentrated his four divisions to attack Planchenois, and Ziethen was advancing with Blucher towards Ohain, along the vast forest of Soignes, where there existed no possible route, by which to turn on Brussels in case of a reverse.

What resolution would Blucher and his counsellors have taken, if the alarming reports of Grouchy's artillery had, about five o'clock, thundered between Moustier and St. Lambert? That is the question. To halt and receive an attack, in a position at once open and dangerous, would have been not only to lose all the fruits of a skillful and bold manoeuvre, but a piece of folly that would have *compromitted* the Prussian army in a perfect cut-throat position. Blucher had, then, but three courses to choose from:

1st. To retrograde without delay on the road that leads from Wavre to Brussels;

2nd. To halt his columns and at once direct them on the Dyle, to dispute Grouchy's passage;

3rd. To precipitate his movement on Ohain and Planchenois, so as to hasten the so much desired junction with Wellington's army, a union that was his first aim, and became his only safe course, when once he found himself engaged in such a situation.

Notwithstanding the manifest advantages of this last, it appears that Blucher, informed of the appearance of the heads of Excelmans' and Vandamme's columns on the heights of Corbaix, and fearing to see them debouch by Moustier, decided on the second; as he suspended Pirch's march, and ordered Ziethen to fall back on the Dyle. It is even asserted, that these troops did not commence their movement till after a report from Thielmann, announcing that the French columns were extending themselves towards Wavre.

We will be permitted to believe, however, that in either case, the Prussian marshal, after having reconnoitred Grouchy's force, had judged the eight divisions of Pirch and Thielmann sufficient to hold it in check, while with the eight divisions of Ziethen and Bulow he would aid Wellington in obtaining the victory.

Be that as it may, it is evident, that the sole appearance of Grouchy towards Moustier had placed the Prussian generals in a really embarrassing position, upon the consequences and gravity of which no one can decide; because all the reasoning that can be brought to bear on this subject, is limited to vague conjectures, for judging of the moral effect which this event had produced on the Prussian generals and their troops.

We cannot deny, however, that if General Gérard's advice was not entirely equivalent to the resolution of advancing on Moustier at daybreak, Marshal Grouchy ought to regret his not deciding on following it. He would have done at least all that it was possible for man to do, to prevent a catastrophe which has unhappily been imputed to him. His bravery and zeal had been tested, he had often given proofs of talent, but he here lost the opportunity of placing his name among the number of most able generals, by labouring to follow strictly the orders that had been given him, it is said, with a little bitterness, and the letter of which he endeavoured to execute, instead of interpreting the spirit of it.

In fact, means for his justification are not wanting; the most important and the best established of all is, that unable to divine Blucher's intentions, and supposing him concentrated in front of Wavre towards Dion le Mont, Grouchy might fear to lay entirely open the communications of the army, by thus throwing himself into the environs of St. Lambert, leaving all the Prussian army behind him. The over-excited partisans of Napoleon have judged his lieutenant with extreme rigor, not dreaming that a portion of the blame should fall on their hero, who had not given him orders entirely satisfactory; and it must be admitted, that there exist but few generals who would have resolved to throw themselves thus on St. Lambert, without knowing what Blucher's main force would undertake.

While the French were committing these faults, their adversaries executed one of the most wise and daring manoeuvres.

The Prussian marshal, who had bivouacked with all his forces about Wavre, on the night of the 17th, had sent, as has been already stated, his chief of staff, Gneisenau, to the Duke of Wellington, to contrive their ulterior operations. It was agreed, that if Napoleon burst upon the English, these should give him battle in front of Waterloo, in the position which their general had reconnoitred eight days previously, in order to cover Brussels if necessary; in this case, Blucher, favoured by the Dyle and the direction of its course, should join him and take part in the battle, by falling on the French right; under the contrary supposition, that is to say, if Napoleon marched on the Prussians to attack them at Wavre, is was agreed that Wellington should act on the same concentric principle, and fall on their left.

Perceiving by the false direction of Grouchy's march, and by the reports of his flankers, that Napoleon was bearing against the English, and that he could without fear fly to his assistance, Blucher caused the corps of Bulow and Pirch to depart for St. Lambert at four o'clock on the morning of the 18th, and himself with Ziethen's, marched on Ohain in order to join the left of the English general. Thielmann was left with 25,000 men at Wavre to defend the Dyle, with instructions to follow the other corps, if Grouchy did not make his appearance. This plan was very well conceived, and it is necessary to say, in praise of the allied generals, that in these combinations is recognized, all the progress they had made in the art of war.

In conformity with these wise dispositions, Bulow was proceeding through Wavre, between seven and eight o'clock in the morning, when a violent conflagration burst forth in the principal street of this city, which was the only passageway; the advanced-guard having already cleared this burning defile, continued on its route; but his artillery not being able to follow, the column busied itself in extinguishing the flames. About noon, the advanced-guard formed at St. Lambert, and awaited the arrival of the corps, that debouched between three and four o'clock from the environs of Pijeau; Pirch's corps had reached beyond Lasne, between five and six o'clock; Blucher, advancing with Ziethen, had made several counter-marches, which prevented him from attaining Ohain before seven o'clock in the evening. We are already aware of the part which these 65,000 Prussians took in the Battle of Waterloo, while Thielmann's corps, posted on the heights of Bierge, overlooking Wavre, and the whole valley of the Dyle, was making his dispositions for opposing Grouchy with a wall of brass, when he should make his appearance.

Arriving in front of Wavre, at four o'clock, this marshal formed his troops to attack the forces left to dispute with him the crossing of the Dyle, which presented a very difficult defile at this point. At five o'clock, he received the orders directed to him that morning at Gembloux; Grouchy then sent Pajol with 8,000 men on Limale, attacked Thielmann's detachment with the remainder of his forces, and debouched, after a very brisk combat, which extended beyond Wavre and the mills of Bierge. The details of this combat, very honourable to both parties, and in which Gérard was wounded, should not form part of our summary.

What was taking place at Mont-St.-Jean rendered, moreover, this success more hurtful than useful. The debris of Napoleon's army regained Genape in horrible disorder; in vain did the staff strive to form it into corps; everything was pell-mell. It would be unjust to reproach the troops for this; never had they fought with more valour, and the cavalry especially had surpassed itself; but, little habituated to seeing themselves thus turned and nigh being enveloped; having exhausted all their munitions and forces, they thought it their duty to seek safety in the most precipitous retreat. Each one wishing to retake the road he had previously followed, they crossed each other in different directions, some to reach the road to Charleroi, others to secure that leading to Nivelle, and escape from the enemy that already appeared on the former; the confusion was complete.

The chief of Blucher's staff, a man of head and heart, was, notwithstanding the night, ordered in pursuit of this tumultuous crowd with the Prussian cavalry that had been less engaged; he appeared unexpectedly before Genape, into which he threw a few shot and shell, and this gave the finishing stroke to the rout. The disorder was so much the greater, as the avenues of this defile had been barricaded to cover the parks that had remained there; and this precaution, so often neglected by the French, turned, under these circumstances, against them, by encumbering the only remaining passageway; this augmented the confusion and doubled the loss of materiel. Grouchy, on his part, being compromised beyond the Dyle, by the very success he had just gained, had only time to throw himself in all haste on Namur, in order to secure the route to Givet and Mézières, and the Prussians failed to prevent him.

The vanquished army had lost 200 pieces of ordnance, and 30,000 men *hors de combat* or prisoners; as many more remained, independently of Grouchy's 35,000 men; but the difficulty was to rally them in presence of an enemy, that had taken lessons in audacity and activity from Napoleon himself. The loss of the allies was not less considerable, but there remained to them 150,000 men,[58] the confidence of victory, and the certainty of being seconded by 300,000 allies, who were crossing the Rhine from Mentz to Bäle.

Such was the issue of this struggle, commenced under such happy auspices, and which resulted more fatal to France than the battles of Poitiers and Azincourt. It must be admitted, that this disaster was the work of a multitude of unheard-of circumstances: if Napoleon can be reproached for certain faults, it must be allowed that fortune dealt cruelly with him in the lesser details, and that his enemies in return, were as fortunate as they showed themselves skilful. However unjust be the spirit of party, we are forced to render homage to the merits of two generals, who, unexpectedly attacked in their cantonments extending from Dinant and Liége to Renaix, near Tournay, had taken such wise measures, as to be in condition next morning for giving battle to equal forces, and for afterwards conquering by an able concentration of the two armies.

As to Napoleon, we have already pointed out the faults in execution, committed the 16th and 17th, as well by himself as by his lieutenants. In the very battle of Waterloo, the French might be censured for having attempted the first attack in masses too deep. This system was never successful against the murderous fire of English infantry and artillery.[59] I have already stated, on the subject of the battle of Esling,

---

58. Besides the troops engaged at Waterloo, the allies had a splendid English division advancing from Ostend, a division encamped at Hall, and Kleist's Prussian corps, that had taken no part in the battle, without mentioning other armies.

59. It is probable that this kind of formation had not been ordered by Napoleon; we have never learned, that he concerned himself about prescribing the manner in which his lieutenants should form their troops, to lead them to an attack. In 1813 alone, he prescribed the columns of battalions by divisions in two ranks, very different from these heavy masses, and such that General Jomini has proposed it in his different works.

(in a former volume,) all that can be said in this respect; but even supposing that this system be suitable on a dry and an open field, easy of access, and with equal artillery force, it is certain, that infantry masses, hurled over muddy ground, from which it is difficult to emerge, with an insufficient concurrence of other arms,[60] attacking troops posted in excellent positions, have many chances against them. Besides, they might also be blamed for not having sufficiently supported this first effort, which, executed without the assistance of the cavalry and reserves, became a partial and isolated movement, and consequently without result.

There were likewise extraordinary charges of cavalry, which being devoid of support, became heroic but useless struggles. Notwithstanding all this, it is almost certain that Napoleon would have remained master of the field of battle, but for the arrival of 65,000 Prussians on his rear; a decisive and disastrous circumstance, that to prevent was not entirely in his power. As soon as the enemy led 130,000 men on the battlefield, with scarcely 50,000 to oppose them, all was lost.

It is time, however, to quit the field of conjecture, and return to the debris of Napoleon's army.

The appearance of the Prussian cavalry, and the cannonade with which it opened on Genape, in the middle of the night, was a circumstance altogether novel in war, where night ordinarily puts a stop to carnage and pursuit. General Gneisenau thought this innovation without danger, against a disbanded army, and was not mistaken, as all took the Charleroi road in great disorder, without waiting for day; and it was only under the guns of Avesnes, that it became possible to rally the battalions and reorganize them a little.

Napoleon had but one course left him, which was to direct Grouchy through the Ardennes on Laon, to collect at this point all that could be drawn from the interior, from Metz and from Rapp's corps, leaving but garrisons in Lorraine and Alsace. The imperial cause was very much shaken, but not entirely lost; should all Frenchmen determine on opposing Europe with the courage of the Spartans of Leonidas, the energy of the Russians in 1812, or of the Spaniards of Palafox. Unfortunately for them, as for Napoleon, opinion was very

---

60. The French had numerous batteries on their front, but they battered the enemy's lines from a distance, and vaguely, and could not easily follow the assailing troops; while the English artillery remaining in position fired muzzle to muzzle, against the columns advancing upon them, and which offered themselves victims to a concentric fire, directed on a single point.

much divided on this subject, and the majority still believing that the struggle interested only the power of the emperor and his family, the fate of the country seemed of little consequence.

Prince Jerome had collected 25,000 men in rear of Avesnes: he was ordered to lead them to Laon; there remained 200 pieces of artillery, beside those of Grouchy.

It required eight days for this marshal to reach Laon: the emperor repaired to that city to await him, persuaded that Wellington, prudent as he had been in Spain, would fear to involve himself, in the midst of so many strong fortresses, and would advance with caution on the Somme.

Napoleon did not admire what are called counsels of war; but under serious circumstances, he loved to reason with some of his familiars for and against the different plans he should follow, and after having listened to all their advice, usually formed his resolution, without even communicating it to those he had called together.

Reaching Laon on the 19th, where he had at first resolved to await the junction of Grouchy and Jerome, the emperor discussed, with the small number of the trustworthy who had followed him, the course he should adopt after this frightful disaster. Should he repair to Paris, and concert with the chambers and his ministers, or else remain with the army, demanding of the chambers to invest him with dictatorial power and an unlimited confidence, under the conviction, that he would obtain from them the most energetic measures, for saving France and conquering her independence, on heaps of ruins?

As it always happens, his generals were divided in opinion; some wished him to proceed to Paris, and deposit the crown into the hands of the nation's delegates, or receive it from them a second time, with the means of defending it. Others, with a better appreciation of the views of the deputies, affirmed, that far from sympathizing with Napoleon, and seconding him, they would accuse him of having lost France, and would endeavour to save the country by losing the emperor. A grave circumstance gave weight to this opinion; it was, that on the very day when he triumphed at Ligny, the elective chamber factiously usurped the initiative right, by adopting a law, ordering the reunion of the institutions scattered through the different constitutions of the consulate and empire. Lastly, the most prudent thought, that Napoleon should not go to Paris, but remain at the head of the army, in order to treat with the sovereigns himself, by offering to abdicate in favour of his son.

It is said, that Napoleon inclined to the idea of remaining at Laon with the army; but the advice of the greatest number determined him, and he departed for Paris. In fact, this was certainly the most efficacious means for concerting with all the authorities, ministers and administrations, on the prompt and vigorous measures necessary to be adopted, in order to organize a grand national resistance; because the Emperor could accomplish more in a few hours himself, than by a hundred despatches. But to succeed, he had to find more ability, disinterestedness and devotion in the chambers than they had yet exhibited.

However, his departure being decided upon, Napoleon repaired to Paris during the night of the 21st June. This, so natural a return, was ill-interpreted; his defeat had lessened him in the eyes of the multitude, who so rarely view things in their true light: they considered his departure from the army as an act of weakness. He had proved, at Arcola, Eylau, Ratisbonne, Arcis, and also at Waterloo, that he was not afraid of bullets; and had he not believed in the resources of France, he would have died at the head of the remains of his army: he quitted them, because he had not a general of his rear-guard who could not lead them to Laon as well as himself, while no one could replace him at the helm of the vessel of state, which, for the instant, was not at his headquarters, but at the Tuileries.

In eight or ten days, he hoped to be on his return to Laon, at the head of 100,000 men, with 400 pieces of artillery, and chastise the Anglo-Prussians for their invasion. Undoubtedly this would not have rid him of the grand armies, which the allied sovereigns were leading by the Vosges: nevertheless, he would have gained time; and if 300,000 men were assembled on the Loire during July, France might yet conquer her independence, and preserve her glory, for many nations have lifted themselves up from a lower depth. The following picture of his situation, traced by Napoleon himself, proves that he was far from despairing:

> So far, Paris could finish her preparations for defence, those at Lyons were completed. The principal fortresses were commanded by chosen officers, and guarded by faithful troops. All could be retrieved, but it required character, energy and absolute devotion on the part of the government, the chambers and the entire nation. It was necessary, that she should be animated by the sole sentiment of national honour, glory and independence; she should fix her eyes on Rome after the battle of Can-

nae, and not on Carthage after that of Zama! France once assuming this lofty stand, is invincible.

Without recurring to the age of the Scipios, it sufficed to recall the example of Spain in 1808, when the French held her places and her capital, and that of Russia setting Moscow on fire, to escape the consequences of the bloody field of Borodino. It will be asserted, undoubtedly, that the circumstances were very different, and that France was too much exhausted of men, to hope for such a result. Such reasons merit no reply: pusillanimous souls never lack pretexts for immediately submitting, when placed under obligation to conquer or to die. It is not allotted to everyone to feel like the Spartans, and sacrifice all to national glory.

Throwing aside this point of patriotic honour, it was not difficult for the political adversaries of Napoleon to prove, even to his partisans, that the cause of France was for the first time separate from his own. To listen to them,

> . . . . .it would only be at the price of seas of blood and of the most dreadful ravages, that you could clear the soil invaded by 500,000 men, and secure her independence. By submitting to the Bourbons, the same result could be obtained, in a manner less Roman, truly, but more certain, and less cruel to France, already worn out by so many wars.

This language was not heroic, but it was conclusive, and calculated to lead all weak minds. The army and the revolutionary party were inclined to resistance, without being alarmed at the sacrifices it demanded; but the party wished for resistance, for the benefit of demagoguism, and not for the interest of the imperial authority. The leaders were deluded into believing, that they could resist Europe by means of decrees, as in 1793. Lafayette, especially, was of a provoking good nature; he flattered himself, that Europe made war only against the ambition of one man, and that the arms of the sovereigns were harmless in presence of his Gallo-American doctrines; he did not perceive that the days of Mack and Cobourg were in the distant past, and that these were precisely the doctrines upon which the sovereigns had designs.

Great disasters, like volcanoes, are announced by a hollow noise which precedes the explosion. Paris had been agitated, since the 20th June, by most alarming reports that bewildered every one. At the first news of the catastrophe, Fouché had his friends of the two chambers assembled at his house,[61] at the same time that his secret agents noised it throughout Paris, that the abdication of Napoleon could alone save the country.

The leaders of the utopianist party dreaded, undoubtedly with reason, the dissolution of the chambers, because, after the course which some of the deputies had adopted, they felt that the emperor would regard them more as obstacles, than as means of government. It was then agreed, in this secret assembly, to forestall the danger; Lafayette was to bell the cat, by proposing to the chamber, on the next day, to declare itself permanent, and proclaim him a traitor to the country, who would dare to order its dissolution. As a remuneration for this act, qualify it as you will, the *great citizen*, who had accompanied the people from Paris to Versailles in 1789, would be newly honoured with his favourite title of Commanding General of the National Guards of the Kingdom.

While Fouché and his friends were thus plotting Napoleon's overthrow, he, at four o'clock on the morning of the 21st, arrived at the Elysée-Bourbon, where Caulaincourt awaited him with just impatience. Far from speaking of a dissolution, the first words uttered by the emperor announced his idea of convening the two chambers in extraordinary session, in order to depict to them the misfortunes of Waterloo, and demand of them the means for saving France; after which he would hasten to rejoin the army.

It is said, that Caulaincourt expressed his regrets on his leaving it, and his fears that the chambers were little disposed to second him. The ministers, summoned immediately after by the emperor, were invited to give their opinions on the measures to be taken. Napoleon imparted to them his views, his resources, and the need he had of the dictatorship in order to save France; he could seize upon it himself, or receive it from the chambers; this latter would be more legal and more efficacious; but was there a certainty of his obtaining it? The greater number of the ministers thought, that everything depended on the harmonious action of the chambers. Caulaincourt cited the forlorn condition of the country in 1814, as a frightful example of the consequences of a dissolution. Fouché also rested all his hopes on an unreserved confidence in these assemblies, in the bosom of which he wielded an active influence.

Decrès thought, on the contrary, that it was not necessary to de-

---

61. Lafayette, Manuel, Dupont de l'Eure, Flauguergues, Dupin the elder, and Henry Lacoste.

pend upon them. Régnaut de Saint-Jean d'Angely himself, this obsequious and complaisant orator, dared to add to the opinion of the minister of marine, that the chambers would undoubtedly exact a new abdication; he even carried his boldness so far as to insinuate, that if not offered, they ought to exact it. Justly indignant at this, and recalling to mind the 18th *Brumaire*, Lucien demanded that the emperor should dispense with the chambers, and save France by himself alone. Lastly, and it should be said to his praise, Carnot entered more largely into the views of a desperate defence, and of the dictatorship that would furnish the means; he considered it necessary to redeem the soil of France at any cost, and to renew, if needed, all the energy of the committee of public safety of 1793. If he never ranked as a great politician, he at least showed the energy of a Roman.

While these grave questions were discussed at the Elysée, the resolutions, adopted the night before in Fouché's secret assembly, bore their fruit in the chambers; the rumours of a dissolution, perfidiously spread long before the subject had been agitated, and at the very moment when, on the contrary, they were proposing proper harmony with the chambers as the only means of safety, had produced the effect intended by the conspirators. Lafayette had just made the sortie agreed upon with success, and had carried, either through jealousy or the weakness of the deputies, the decree declaring as traitors to the country all those who would dare pronounce a dissolution, though this act was nevertheless one of the constitutional rights of the emperor. Singular mania of these pretended apostles of legality, immolating the chief of state for wishing to execute the law!

This decree, that was, by itself alone, an entire revolution, was transmitted to the assembly of the ministers engaged with Napoleon: henceforth there was nothing more to hope for; in vain did Lucien, accompanied by the ministers, demand of the chambers, in the name of the emperor, to appoint a commission to contrive measures of public safety, indispensable under the circumstances: his abdication was the sole aim of the conspirators. The commission was in truth appointed, but was composed of the warmest enemies of the emperor, Laujuinais, Lafayette, Grenier, Flauguergues, and Dupont de l'Eure; the majority only proposed a foolish and vain negotiation with the powers. At the reading of the report a crowd of deputies, and Lafayette, especially, cried out that this would be insufficient without the abdication; that this abdication or its forfeiture, was necessary within the hour.

While these vociferations of mediocrity and of hatred, staggered moderate minds, Napoleon was at the Elysée, a prey to the most violent agitation. The people assembled about this palace, made the air resound with cries of *vive l'Empereur!* and asked for arms. Lucien urged his brother to profit by this enthusiasm, and enact an 18th *Brumaire*, more legal than the first, because, in ordering the dissolution according to the prescribed forms, he had a right to require it and have it executed.

The idea of saving the country by arming the lower classes against the highest magistracy, must have been revolting to the judicious and lofty spirit of Napoleon. Besides, discord, already so potent in France, would not fail to redouble after a *coup d'etat*, which would recall rather that of May 31st, 1793, than that of the 18th *Brumaire*. The sacred union of the nation and its chief, could alone repair the cruel effects of these bloody disasters; it was then by closing around the celebrated conqueror, that France could still issue gloriously from a gigantic struggle. From the moment the nation divided itself into three hostile camps, and the authorities gave the example of defection, all was lost, because Napoleon could not himself alone, save the independence of the country, as well as his throne. The ideologists and the factious, who were so senseless as to imagine, that Europe would be eager to lay down her arms before their decrees, and who thought of causing the triumph of their Utopias by sacrificing a great man, will alone have to answer for the humiliation they were preparing for themselves.

Repelling, then, the suggestions of his brother, Napoleon preferred to resign, and dictated to Lucien the following abdication in favour of his son:

> Frenchmen! in commencing the war for upholding the national independence, I calculated on the union of all efforts, of all wills, and on the concurrence of all the national authorities; I had reason to hope for success, and I braved all the declarations of the powers against me. Circumstances appear to me changed. I offer myself a sacrifice to the hatred of the enemies of France. May they prove sincere in their declarations, and have really no design but upon my person. My political life is ended, and I proclaim my son, under the title of Napoleon II., emperor of the French. The present ministers will compose the council of the government. The interest I take in my son induces me to invite the chambers, immediately, to pass a law organizing the regency. Let all unite for the public safety, and to continue an independent nation!

We are assured, that the emperor at first intended to send a pure and simple abdication, but that Lucien and Carnot determined him to stipulate in favour of his son. Be that as it may, many have blamed him for this resolution as a weakness. If he had only consulted his own character, he would have buried himself beneath his country's ruins, sooner than have so easily yielded; the long series of combats sustained, after his departure from Moscow, even to the very foot of Montmartre, sufficiently proves it. But how could he share his sentiments with entire France, when the very government had just declared that a second abdication was necessary? Without the concurrence of the country, what could he do? If Napoleon had made the sacrifice of his throne at Fontainblean, when he had greater titles to the devotion of the nation, and when the enemy were less formidable, could he refuse now, when himself and his private interests were alone concerned? Could he consent to a social subversion, and to France being laid waste, in order to satisfy his military vanity? No. . . . His resignation, far from being an act of discouragement, was worthy the rest of his life.

Having decided on going to America, Napoleon hoped that the allies would rest satisfied with the hostage he placed at their discretion, and would leave the crown on the head of the son of Maria Louisa. He thought this was the best means, of effecting the fusion of ancient interests with the new, and preventing a civil war which might again run over the entire circle from 1789 to 1804; but the solemn engagements entered into at Vienna, between the sovereigns and Louis XVIII., did little permit them to consent to such a transaction, which at best had then been excusable, as their object was to prevent the grand struggle that was expected, and the issue of which was not considered so certain or so speedy. Before the war, the sovereigns might have hesitated in effecting the triumph of the principle of legitimacy, by the doubtful force of arms; but once conquerors, how were they to repel it? By what right could they prevent their ally, Louis XVIII., from entering the capital, and resuming the crown?

Besides, Napoleon's precaution in stipulating for his son, remained without result through the singular pre-occupation of the leaders of the chamber, who flattered themselves, with yet dictating laws to France, and having them accepted by Europe. Not wishing to admit Napoleon II., nor establish the regency, they hastened to form a provisional government, in the hope of seizing the helm of state, treating with the allied sovereigns for their existence, and not resuming the government of the Bourbons, but with conditions imposed by the chambers. How absurd a dream in the actual state of affairs! and which would suit neither Louis XVIII., nor the sovereigns armed in the cause of thrones.

Here the task of the historian, who attaches great value to impartiality, becomes not less embarrassing than painful. Indeed, how will he portion out to each one, the meed of blame or praise that pertains to him, in these great political conflicts? Will he treat all the adversaries of Napoleon as sycophants and revolutionists? Will he compare Fouché to Catiline, and will he regard the utopianist deputies, on whom he relied, as so many of the Gracchi; or rather, following in the footsteps of the ignoble Abbé of Montgaillard, will he treat Napoleon and all his partisans as blood-thirsty ogres, dreaming but of devastation and pillage? Will he, like this pamphleteer, raise to the rank of *demi*-gods, all those who contributed to the ruin of the imperial system?

Without thus pushing things to extremes, it will ever be a perplexing matter to qualify Fouché's intrigues; some will state that they were the result of a wise foresight of the ills that threatened France, after the declarations of the Congress at Vienna, as well as a worthy desire of preserving her from too unequal a contest; others will attribute them solely to the ambitious and seditious tendency of his mind, as well as to his still somewhat revolutionary doctrines. Should a minister be stamped as a traitor or receive commendations, who, while preserving his official position towards the chief of state, corresponded and treated clandestinely with his enemies, without authority?

Who will dare award civic crowns to the influential members of the chambers, for their conduct, both before and after the news of the disaster at Waterloo? Will it be credited, that they preserved France from utter ruin, by usurping an authority which the constitution did not give them; or else, will they be accused of having added to the military humiliation of the country, by cowardly abandoning the only captain who was still able to heighten the brightness of her standards, and preserve her independence?

In recapitulating all the disasters that might befall France, by prolonging a struggle *à outrance*, we cannot deny that it was a frightful alternative, and that the result of the course adopted would sufficiently justify the conduct of the chambers, had they always been inspired solely by the interest of the country. However, who can also say, that Napoleon would not have cleared French soil of her enemies, had he been powerfully and freely supported? Who can affirm, that the expenses of the occupation, and the two thousand millions imposed by the allies or paid to the emigrants, had not exceeded, by far, the monetary and transient ravages, the consequences of a few months' struggle?

Though, perhaps, despairing too soon of the public safety, had the chambers at least appreciated the only remedy for the evils that threatened the country, and had boldly proclaimed the recall of the legitimate government, soliciting from the king the proclamation of certain fundamental principles, requisite to reassure minds against a violent reaction, we would have been able to acknowledge some political foresight on the part of their leaders; but all their measures, on the contrary, attest a miserable spirit of mediocrity, of hatred towards the powers of the government, and a liberalism ridiculously vain, which destroyed even the garb of patriotism with which they clothed their declamations? These are grave and immense questions, upon which I do not feel myself called upon to pass judgment, and which I hasten to leave, and return to the emperor.

Still full of the souvenirs of 1813 and 1814, Europe did not at all comprehend the rapidity of this second fall. The empire of Carthage, likewise crumbled at Zama; because the Carthagenian hero had, like Napoleon, lost his influence in the heart of the country. The monarchy of Frederic the Great fell as rapidly at Jéna, but owed her existence to the principle of legitimacy, so ill appreciated by declaimers; Frederic William, happier than Hannibal and Napoleon, had left his nation in mourning and preserved the love of his people. In this great wreck, Napoleon could, nevertheless, exclaim, with Francis I.: *All is lost, save honour.*

Napoleon did not quit France, till the enemy neared his retreat at Malmaison. Informed of his abdication, and of the anarchy that had succeeded him, and even prompted, as it is asserted, by Fouché, the Anglo-Prussians had advanced rapidly on Paris; they could have outstripped Grouchy, but they followed closely on his steps. Wellington had carried Péronne and Cambrai at the first onset, where pitiable citizens ignominiously aided him. The rapidity of this invasion fully proved, that Europe had not forgotten the lessons given by Napoleon himself.

Meanwhile, the Prussians made a hazardous movement, in seeking to turn the works erected to the north of Paris; they alone crossed the Seine near Pecq, while Wellington remained on the right bank, and, from his position, unable to support them. The army, then commanded by Davoust, and encamped in the vicinity, might have fallen upon them with 70,000 brave men, and annihilated them by tumbling them into the Seine. Napoleon proposed to the provisional government, to take command of the army, and resign the same after having conquered. Vile intrigues prevented him from washing out the stain of Waterloo, and taking leave of France after a victory, that had permitted him to treat honourably with the allied sovereigns, instead of surrendering at discretion to an English general and a Prussian marshal, as was done by the provisional government. Far from accepting his proposition, Fouché, who was already corresponding with Wellington, had even resolved, for fear he would of his own accord put himself at the head of the army, to secure his person and place him in a species of captivity, by confiding him to the guard of General Becker.

Nevertheless, the enthusiasm of the troops was still so great, that this deplorable government had great difficulty in causing a suspension of hostilities, and General Excelmans even destroyed an entire brigade near Ville-d'Avray, at the moment when they were enchaining the courage of his comrades.

The emperor left for Rochefort immediately afterwards. Decrés the minister, proposed to him to leave from Havre, on an American vessel ready to set sail; but this was too near the English coast, and he was also rather late. He could also have embarked at Bordeaux, on the one chartered by Joseph: the objections to a disagreeable counsellor diverted him from it; fearing to fall into the hands of his enemies in a commercial port, he determined to go aboard a public ship, but some of the factious had time to forewarn the English of the fact.[62] Joseph embarked alone at Bordeaux, and reached America without interruption, on the vessel which he had offered to his brother. The latter was less fortunate: closely pressed by the English cruiser on his leaving Rochefort, and seeing that it would be difficult to escape, he pushed directly for her, hoping to place himself under the safeguard of British honour and British laws. He wrote the following letter to the Prince Regent:

> Your royal highness: exposed to the factions that divide my country, and to the enmity of the greatest European powers, I have terminated my political career. Like Themistocles, I come to sit at the hearth of the British people. I place myself under the protection of their laws, which I demand of your royal

---

62. The *History of the Restoration* asserts positively, that Fouché informed Wellington of this embarkation, and so contrived it, that the emperor should not escape.

highness, as from the most powerful, the most constant, and the most generous of my adversaries.

This letter, remarkable for the simplicity of its style, and for the just comparison established, between the position of Napoleon and that of the illustrious Athenian, could not disarm the hatred of his enemies. His was a cruel disappointment. It has been thought, that he would have been treated very differently, had he presented himself at the headquarters of the emperor Alexander, trusting his fate to the magnanimity of his sentiments. Had this monarch considered it necessary, for the repose of Europe, to confine his formidable antagonist in one of his palaces, he would have treated him, at least, with all the consideration that was due him, and not with the barbarity of the unworthy jailor, that England gave him.

Posterity will judge of the treatment he suffered. Prisoner in another hemisphere, nothing was left him, but to defend the reputation that history was preparing for him, and which was still being perverted according to the passions of parties. Death surprised him while writing his commentaries, which have remained imperfect, and this was, no doubt, one of his greatest regrets. However, he can repose in peace; pigmies cannot obscure his glory; he has gathered, in the victories of Montenotte, Castiglione, Arcola, Rivoli, the Pyramids, as well as in those of Marengo, Ulm, Austerlitz, Jéna, Friedland, Abensburg, Ratisbonne, Wagram, Borodino, Bautzen, Dresden, Champ-Aubert, Montmirail, and Ligny, laurels sufficient to efface the disaster of Waterloo; his five codes will be titles not less honourable, to the suffrages of posterity. The monuments erected in France and in Italy, will attest his greatness to the remotest ages.

His adversaries have reproached him with a tendency to an oriental despotism, and I shared this opinion with them for a long time: only true statesmen should judge him in this respect; what seemed a crime to the eyes of utopianists, will someday become, to the eyes of enlightened men, his most glorious title to wisdom and foresight. With hollow and abstract ideas, or a philanthropic sentimentality, a great nation will never march on to high destinies, or even, be able victoriously to defend herself, against formidable neighbours.

The great European communities, whatever be said by all the Don Quixottes of governmental metaphysics, will never be but egotistical and rival communities.[63] Therefore, all well-ordered communities

---

63. This truth, which appears simple by being, evident, has very singularly been unrecognized in these latter times, because the celebrated (continued next page.)

should invest their chiefs with all the power indispensable for rendering them formidable abroad and respected at home. Without these conditions, there will exist in his government but anarchy, demagoguism or weakness. According to the Utopias of Lafayette, Lanjuinais, and B. Constant, we should only make *citizen kings*, without dignity and without power, like those of Poland or Hungary; or else anarchical republics, like those of the year 4 and the year 5. All subtle declamations could not weaken this great truth.—That with the license of the press and popular elections, no continental power would exist fifty years; and France less than any other, thanks to the passionate and impetuous spirit of the nation. Experience will finally prove who best understood his true interests, Napoleon or the doctrinaires who undermined his power.

Some men, blinded by their utopias, have pretended " that he had alienated from himself the enlightened classes of Frenchmen, by smothering thought; that he had, *by striking it with a magic sceptre*, arrested the moral and political progress of the human species, which was compressed under an enormous weight, and retained in woeful immobility." These grand phrases have fascinated little minds; but the suffrages of sensible men will remain to him, and the next generation will justly appreciate, whether the shamelessness of thought, and the press is not more to be dreaded, for a nation like the French, than the bounds he wished to place to their license;[64] they will see whether the public morals and the national character, will have gained much by the rupture of all checks; whether the right to *say everything, print everything, and vilify everything*, will form great men, and will cause real progress in human reason, or rather, whether the result of this pretended golden age be not all the reverse.

As to the charge of unbridled and unbounded ambition, which we ourselves have not spared him, it must be admitted that appearances at least condemned him: however, we have not sufficiently considered

---

author of the *Letters on the hundred days*, in speaking of Napoleon's fall, has attributed it to the hatred that commerce bore him, which, according to the publicist, *tends to efface rivalry between nations, and to draw together individuate as well as nations:* strange doctrine, that denotes an inconceivable ignorance of the history of all ages, as if the great struggles of Carthage and Rome, as well as those between England, France, and Holland, only sprung from the rivalry of merchants, more tenacious even than feudal or national rivalry.

64. We cannot too often repeat that the imperial censorship, absurd in its regulating dispositions, would have been good in itself, if it had extended only over the periodical press, and had been confided to men more independent by their position.

the necessities of his position, as well towards England as towards the other European powers, and especially towards the emigrant princes of the revolution. Many invasions and aggressions were dictated by these necessities.

The idea of a grand European domination, in opposition to the English power, certainly led him beyond all bounds of wisdom and moderation, and powerfully contributed to his fall; but if this idea was a lofty one, and worthy of him, it is just to say that the means he employed for accomplishing his ends, were revolting to his allies, and did him more injury than the projects themselves.

Here ends our task; this small work having for its object, but the completion of the life of Napoleon, related by himself, we have not considered it our duty to narrate the sequel of the invasion, which followed the battle of Waterloo, and the departure of the emperor. Everybody is aware of the convention concluded on the 3rd July, by Davoust and the delegates of the provisional government, for the evacuation of Paris and the retreat of the army behind the Loire. We cannot, however, refrain from citing the heroic defence of Huningue, by General Barbanégre with a handful of mutilated veterans, and the glorious combat sustained in Savoy, by Colonel Bujeaud, with his single regiment, against an entire division of the Austrians, in which he made more prisoners than he had soldiers; an isolated feat of arms, but which attested the spirit which animated the army.

Lastly, we will also recall the fact, that the chambers received the reward of their deplorable conduct. The commissioners they sent to the sovereigns were scarcely admitted at headquarters, and after certain conferences, were informed, that there was no occasion for treating with them: finally, a picket of Prussian *landwehrs*, posted one beautiful morning at the door of their chamber to prevent their assembling, taught the deputies the vanity and puerility of their pretensions.

A few days subsequently, Louis XVIII. quietly entered the Tuileries; prompted by the most excited royalists, he at first yielded to the most violent reactionary ideas; but France and Europe did not delay in raising their voices against the folly of this exaggerated course. The world knows what took place after the death of this sage and paternal monarch, and how the revolution of 1830 proved, that the return from Elba was not so extravagant as had been imagined. In truth, the results to the country were frightful; the foreign occupation continued to 1818, the loss of many important fortresses, the two thousand millions paid to the allies and emigrants, the military humiliation, worse, perhaps, than all these, such were the sad results of a resolution which Napoleon would have abstained from taking, had he been able to have foreseen the consequences.

The reports that the allied sovereigns had quitted Vienna, little satisfied with the proceedings of the congress, the rumour of a project on foot for removing him from Elba, and exiling him far from Europe,—lastly, the famous discourse of Ferrand, of which we have spoken, were the three grand motives that led him to this bold attempt; if the departure of the sovereigns had been confirmed, everything leads us to the belief that he would have succeeded; because he would have had time to negotiate, on the one hand, and on the other, to place the entire nation under arms.

Such is the weakness of human calculations, that the most astounding enterprise that has ever been conceived, succeeded, at first, against all probabilities and appearances, then miscarried in another which, proving false, destroyed all chances of success. We are undoubtedly authorized in believing, that victory at the battle of Waterloo by Napoleon, would have rendered the struggle still long and terrible; but it would require a great share of credulity to be persuaded, that he could have prevented the 350,000 allies that crossed the Rhine between Bäle and Manheim, from pushing forward to Paris; because Napoleon, being compelled to leave from sixty to eighty thousand men in Belgium, against Blucher and Wellington, could not have assembled 100,000 on the Moselle or the Vosges. Now, Paris being occupied, what course would France have pursued, thus divided in opinion, and placed between two chiefs, dethroned in fact? Would she have imitated Spain, and continued a national war *à outrance*, as desired by Napoleon and Carnot?

If the coalition had had to open partial negotiations between London, Berlin, Petersburg and Vienna, Napoleon would have had four months more in which to arm, and without doubt would have succeeded in detaching one or other of the powers. This was then his principal chance of success.

As to the chances of war, we have seen that Ney's delay on the 15th and 16th June; that caused by Napoleon in the reconnoissance made and in the measures adopted for attacking Blucher's army; the vague and tardy direction assigned to Grouchy; finally, the false route taken by the latter, on the morning of the 18th, were the leading causes of the disaster at Waterloo. Some military men have also thought, that Napoleon would have succeeded better by not throwing himself between the allied armies, as this gave to each the possibility of assembling completely; they believe that he should have fallen either on Blucher's centre, by Namur, or on Wellington's, by Ath or Mons. It is certain that by this means, he would have cut off one or other of these enemies; if he had beaten the centre and left of Wellington's cantonments, the right would have retreated in the direction of Ostend or Antwerp; had he overthrown the centre of Blucher's cantonments, the left would have been forced on Liége, and hence the junction of these disjointed parts had been quite impossible.

But both of these projects offered difficulties; to fall by Florette, between Charleroi and Namur, that is to say, between the corps of Ziethen and Pirch, there was the very difficult ground situated at the mouth of the Sambre; besides, the troops arriving from French Flanders would have to defile during more than one day, in front of the enemy's cantonments. By falling on Braine, or Ath, the centre of the English cantonments, the corps of the Prince of Orange could not be prevented from joining Blucher with all the troops on the left; now, 120,000 Prussians, increased to 180,000 by the half of Wellington's army and a portion of Kleist's corps, might still be in condition to dispute the Meuse against 120,000 French. Chances multiply *ad infinitum*, when we abandon ourselves to gratuitous suppositions, in the field. The plan of operations adopted was so much the most favourable, that without the time lost, on the 16th and the morning of the 17th, he would have succeeded completely, and that even this loss of time would have been regained on the 18th, had the right wing taken the direction of Moustier.

Appendix

The Duke of Elchingen, son of Marshal Ney, having made certain observations on the faults imputed to his father, in this campaign of Waterloo, the Author has replied in the following letter, that throws a new light on these important events:

Monsieur Le Duc,
I have carefully read and considered the observations you have done me the honour of addressing me, on my *political and military summary* of the campaign of 1815, printed two years since, but not yet published.

While I render full justice to the filial sentiments that prompt you, to remove the reproaches heaped on your father, for the de lays in occupying Quatre-Bras, during the 15th and 16th June, I ought also to render justice to the frankness and impartiality that prevail in all your researches, and to the convictions that animate you.

You must have noticed in my narrative, that I expressed real doubts as to what occurred relative to Quatre-Bras, up to nine o'clock on the morning of the 16th, the hour when, it is said, General Flahaut left Charleroi with *written* orders for him to take possession of it. These doubts have not appeared entirely satisfactory to you, and you would wish me to share all your convictions, which, in view of the numerous contradictions that are evident from the published documents, is not without difficulty.

Napoleon and General Gourgaud affirm, under circumstances, that seem by their nature to merit confidence, that a previous order to occupy this important position, had been given verbally to the commander of the left wing, on the night of the 15th.

To these assertions, you oppose:

1st. A letter from the major-general, that speaks of Gosselies, and not of Quatre-Bras;

2nd. The expressions and date of the letter dictated to General Flahaut, on the 16th;

3rd. Your conversation with Marshal Soult in 1829;

4th. The declaration of General Heymès, an eyewitness;

5th. A declaration of General Reille, setting forth, that at seven o'clock on the morning of the 16th, Marshal Ney had said to him, that he was awaiting orders; from which you conclude that he had not yet received any.

Your reasons are powerful, *Monsieur le Duc* however, the last one especially, might also be differently explained; the marshal could very well have received verbal orders during the night, and yet say to General Reille that he still awaited them, because he might suppose, that important modifications would occur in the emperor's combination, in consequence of reports he had just made him, according to his own statement.

My great familiarity with war operations and the duties of the staff, induces me to give you a sketch of the manner in which, it seems to me, these things must have happened, without pretending, however, to set myself up as judge in this great debate, and without renewing the recital of operations already to be found in my volume.

Debouching from Charleroi, with his whole army, Napoleon had before him, two causeways, forming nearly a right angle, that is to say, going in directions entirely divergent, one to the north on Brussels, and the other to the east on Namur, Wellington being at the former and Blucher at the latter. The route from Charleroi to Brussels, being at once on the extreme left of the cantonments of the Anglo-Netherlanders, and on the extreme right of the Prussian cantonments, was evidently the point where the junction of the two armies should take place. A crossroad that connects these two causeways, runs directly from Namur to Brussels, and into Hainault; it passes through Sombref, joins the Brussels' causeway at Quatre-Bras, and thus forms the base of a triangle, of which Charleroi is the vertex.

With the slightest glance at the map, you perceive that in occupying Sombref, the Prussians from Namur are prevented from joining the English, the same as in occupying Quatre-Bras, you prevent the English from Nivelles and Brussels from joining the Prussians. This double combination could not escape the eagle eye of Napoleon: it is also averred, that he gave Grouchy a verbal order to push, if possible, as far as Sombref on the 15th. Should we not conclude from this, that he must also have made known to the commander of the left wing, his desire that he should push on to Quatre-Bras, this decisive point being nearer Reille's corps than Sombref was to Grouchy's troops?

As for myself, I think I am too well aware of Napoleon's genius, to doubt his conceiving, on the 15th June, the idea of having Quatre-Bras occupied, and even previous to the assertions from St. Helena, I could not express the least thought to the contrary, though the declaration of the Duke of Dalmatia, cited in your pamphlet, has raised doubts in my mind.[1]

Admitting, then, the existence of this verbal order of the 15th, the main point would still be to know, in what terms it was couched. Did he prescribe to the marshal, *to rush headlong upon all he should find in this direction*, as is affirmed in book 9. from St. Helena? or else, limit himself to recommending, as he did to Grouchy, as rapid a march as possible on the route to Brussels, taking care to throw forward his advance-guard on Quatre-Bras? The order having been given verbally, it would be very difficult to decide between these two hypotheses; but all the information given in your pamphlet, and all that took place on the 16th, authorize us in admitting the second version. In that case, I believe we would be justified in drawing from this fact, different conclusions from those that have been admitted heretofore; the following are the reasons:

Vandamme's and Gérard's infantry, having been retarded on the 15th, by incidents unnecessary to recall, and Grouchy having only cavalry with him, was stopped towards Gilly by two divisions of Prussian infantry, so that instead of advancing as far as Sombref, he was not even able to occupy Fleurus, held by Ziethen's troops. Marshal Ney, finding himself, then, with

---

1. The Duke of Dalmatia declares, in this conversation, that the order for the occupation of Quatre-Bras was not issued on the night of the 15th, but only on the 16th, after the emperor had breakfasted. It could be, however, possible, that a verbal order had been given on the 15th, without the major-general's presence, and even without his knowledge.

Reille's corps, beyond Gosselies, ought, very naturally, to hesitate in throwing himself on Quatre-Bras, with three divisions, before being joined by d'Erlon's corps, that was with difficulty debouching from Marchiennes; because the cannonade of the combat at Gilly, that thundered audibly in his rear, might render this movement dangerous.

In truth, decisive circumstances sometimes present themselves in war, when it is not necessary to be too much alarmed at what is passing in the rear, (witness the little importance attached by the French, to Lusignan's column, debouching in their rear at the Battle of Rivoli); but these cases are exceptions, and as a general rule, we cannot devote too much attention to what the enemy may undertake on our line of retreat. Moreover, Reille threw Girard's division to the right on Heppignies, to cover himself in the direction of Fleurus, where Ziethen concentrated his four infantry divisions, to await Pirch's four divisions, that were to arrive that night. Certainly, if Marshal Ney had had his seven divisions in hand, he could very well have led four on Frasne, and three on Quatre-Bras; but knowing that he could not calculate on d'Erlon's corps that day, and being absolutely ignorant of the position of Wellington's forces, can he be blamed for having hesitated to execute this partial and somewhat eccentric movement, in the midst of two armies, that numbered not less than 220,000 combatants?

For my own part, I do not think so, *unless the order to rush headlong on Quatre-Bras, had been expressed in a formal manner*[2] I go farther, I even believe that Napoleon, on his return to Charleroi, after the combat at Gilly, ought to have congratulated himself, on his left remaining *à la hauteur* of the rest of the army, that bivouacked about Lambusart; because, thus situated, this wing ran no risk, and could, at five o'clock in the morning, depart for Quatre-Bras, while Grouchy rapidly advanced on Sombref.

This, so palpable a fact, bears me out in the belief, that in his interview with Marshal Ney, the night of the 15th and 16th, Napoleon expressed himself to that effect.[3] It is at least quite

---

2. Napoleon wrote at St. Helena from recollection, having no written documents: his memory was a good one, it is true, but when verbal orders, given amid the confusion of an operation such as the passage of the Sambre, are at issue, he may, three years afterwards, have been deceived as to the expressions employed.

3. This is so true, that in book 9 the emperor formally states, that on the night of the 15th, everything had succeeded to his wishes, (continued next page.)

certain, that among the first words they interchanged, the emperor must have entertained the marshal with what had been done, and what was necessary still to do; now, if the former expressed more or less regret that the left had halted between Frasne and Gosselies, the right being towards Lambusart, *he must necessarily have added, either that this delay should be repaired next morning, or that at daybreak he should receive further instructions, such as the reports of the night would demand.*

In fact, if Marshal Ney had not again seen the emperor after the receipt of the order of the 15th, it is clear, that it would have been his duty, at daybreak, to resume its execution, deferred the previous night; because, when operations are carried on at the distance of a march from headquarters, and when a prescribed movement is delayed by certain incidents, it ought, as a matter of course, to be executed as soon as possible, so long as it is not revoked. But as the generals had conferred a long time together, the night subsequent to the non-execution of the order, it was altogether otherwise, and the marshal could regard this anterior order as null and void, if not formally confirmed. We see, then, that the intention manifested by the emperor at this interview, constitutes the knot in the enigma. Which of the two intentions above mentioned, did he express? There lies the whole question; and, if there was no witness to this conference, God alone can decide.

For myself, I can only form an opinion from appearances, or on conjectures: now notice what to my eyes are these appearances, should I properly retrace the emperor's state of mind and the data from which he judged.

Napoleon did not certainly calculate on surprising the allied armies, asleep in their cantonments, that extended from Liége to Malines; but he counted on taking the initiative, and beating them separately, while endeavouring to concentrate. Rapidity was then the first of the elements of victory, but the rapidity of Rivoli, Castiglioni, and especially of Abensburg and Dresden.

The Prussians were the first to be encountered, and their resistance at Gilly intimated, that the main body of their forces was not very distant. This might have determined the emperor not to renew the formal order to march on Quatre-Bras at day-

---

and that his operation promised a certain success; an unaffected avowal of the little value he attached, to the partial and isolated occupation of Quatre-Bras, for that day.

break, before having received the morning reports. Grouchy wrote on the 16th, at six o'clock, that large Prussian columns arriving by the Namur road, were forming towards Ligny; his report, which I have seen, could have arrived at seven; but things do not always move as rapidly as they should, and it is probable that this dispatch did not arrive before nine o'clock. Napoleon had just dictated to General Flahaut, the order to advance on Quatre-Bras, and he stated in this communication, that a similar order had been previously sent by Marshal Soult, but that he dispatched his *aide-de-camp* Flahaut, because he was better mounted than the staff officers, and would reach him sooner.

These precautions certainly attest, that at this moment, the emperor attached great value to the prompt execution of this movement, and authorize the belief that he had conceived the idea at daylight, because he had already prescribed to the Duke of Dalmatia to expedite it, and dictated, at eight o'clock, the confirmation of a previous order. But all this appears, also, to indicate, that in the night conference no similar order had been given to Marshal Ney; if this had happened, so much care would not have been taken to send him a triple order, after eight o'clock in the morning, when he could have already reached Quatre-Bras, had the order been issued at midnight.

This reasoning leads me to the conclusion, that if a first order had actually been given him on the evening of the 15th, the emperor had announced, in the night conference, that he would issue him others the next day; the entire purport of General Flahaut's letter, as well as the saying of Reille, conduces to the belief.

After having done all in my power to clear up the events of the day and night of the 15th, it remains for me to penetrate the mysteries of the morning of the 16th, and at the very outset, I find myself in presence of a very grave circumstance.

Book 9 from St. Helena pretends, that Marshal Ney received *during the night*, the order to advance rapidly on Quatre-Bras, and at the same time declares, that this order was carried by the *aide-de-camp*, General Flahaut. Now, your pamphlet gives a letter from this general, affirming, that the order in question was dictated to him between eight and nine o'clock in the morning, which, in the month of June, is some hours after dawn. In fact, General Flahaut also says that this dictation occurred at an early hour, an expression that astonishes me, as at this period of the year, eight and nine o'clock are not early hours.

I have explained above, how the inference might be drawn, from the very expressions of this dispatch, that it contained the first formal order to occupy Quatre-Bras. One single circumstance, might cause a different interpretation of the facts I have just cited; it is thus stated in the writings from St. Helena, (Book 9):

> Marshal Ney must have suspended his movement on Quatre-Bras a second time, because he had learned that the junction of the two armies was taking place, and thought this might change. the determinations of the emperor, from whom he demanded orders.

We indeed find in your pamphlet, that General Reille called on the marshal at seven in the morning, and that the latter informed him, that he was awaiting the emperor's orders, *to whom he had reported his position.*

It is probable that this fact is the same that is mentioned above; but it is expressed in such a manner, that we cannot conclude in favour or against the marshal, as the report appears to have been made verbally by an officer of the staff, long after the departure of General Flahaut. The orders, dictated first to Marshal Soult, and later to this general, were not then occasioned by this report; and the inferences you can draw from these reiterated dispatches, to prove, that no confirmation of the verbal order of the 15th had been given at night, remain in their full force.

After all, great obscurity prevails over this report of the marshal, as over many other points; book 9 speaks of the arrival of this officer towards Fleurus, just as the Prussian army had been reconnoitred, that is, about noon. Now, the marshal had already stated to Reille, at Gosselies, about seven, that he had rendered an account of his position, and had asked for orders. The officer charged with it had been sent to Charleroi: how was it, that he did not arrive before the emperor's departure?

On the other hand, I find in General Reille's letter, that at nine o'clock he received and expedited directly to the emperor, an officer sent by General Girard, announcing that the entire Prussian army was forming in *rear of Fleurus*. One hour afterwards, Marshal Soult writes from Charleroi to the commander of the left wing, that an officer of lancers has just reported, that large masses of the enemy appear in *the direction of Quatre-Bras*. This last was written at ten o'clock, and coincides with the sending of the officer from Girard. This, perhaps, might be the suspending report, mentioned. On the other hand, how could the emperor confound Quatre-Bras and Fleurus, while answering the report of the officer sent by Reille?[4] And when he had inserted in the same dispatch, that Blucher having passed the night at Namur, his army could detach no portion on Quatre-Bras, was Napoleon ignorant of what Grouchy, Girard and Reille had reported, or else, placed he more faith in his secret agents who gave him contrary information? This is what the most skilful would be unable to explain. Finally, it is unfortunate, that this report attributed to the marshal, has not come down to us in manuscript; it would have cleared up many doubts respecting the orders previously given.

But let us throw aside all the suppositions to which these divers incidents would give rise, and return to facts. General Reille writes from Gosselies, at a quarter after ten o'clock, that General Flahaut has communicated to him the orders with which he was charged for the marshal, which presupposes that these orders passed Gosselies about ten, and reached Frasne about eleven, as Colonel Heymes states. General Reille adds, "that in the absence of Ney, he suspends his march on Quatre-Bras, because very recent information, as to the arrival of great Prussian masses, appears to him of a nature to change the emperor's dispositions; he therefore awaits a positive order from the marshal."

This incident, which was certainly a misfortune, occasioned a new delay, but this was not a decisive event, after what had taken place at Fleurus and Ligny. In fact, it is evident, that if the marshal did not receive the order at Frasne, before eleven o'clock, and if Reille awaited the result of it before placing himself in motion, he could not well move before noon; therefore, there was no possibility of commencing the attack at Quatre-Bras before two, as it actually happened. Now, at noon, the

---

4. This may seem strange, but is not at all impossible: preoccupied with the thought, that Reille was advancing towards Quatre-Bras against the English, Napoleon perhaps imagined, that the assembling of the army reported by the officer sent by this general, was only a portion of the English army, that was to cover Quatre-Bras.

Prussian army in rear of Ligny had just been reconnoitred, and it was rather late to advance on Genape, when it had become necessary to march on Bry: it would have been better, to have established the half of the left in position in front of the Prince of Orange, to mask this corps, and disposed of the other half for completing the defeat of the Prussians, a manoeuvre that the previous delays did not prevent them from executing.

We indeed know, that if the first and most important of the principles of war is, to concentrate the main body of the forces to strike a decisive blow on a portion of the enemy's line, there is a second which is the complement of it: it is, not to compromise the weak wing, on the contrary, to refuse it in such a manner, that it cannot engage in an unequal struggle. A serious engagement at Quatre-Bras, was then a real misfortune at that hour.

For the rest, *Monsieur le Duc*, I refer you to my work, where I have frankly stated what I thought of this uncertainty, that has reigned throughout the morning of the 16th; and as I perceive that I have already written to too great a length, I will endeavour, as well as in me lies, to recapitulate amid so many contradictions.

1st. It appears to me evident, that from the 15th, Napoleon expressed the desire that Quatre-Bras, as well as Sombref, should be occupied. But as the right could not advance beyond Lambusart, the night of the 15th, it is probable, that he was satisfied with the left remaining between Frasne and Gosselies.

2nd. In every state of the case, the delay caused to this occupation on the 15th, was of no consequence, as it sufficed that it should take place on the 16th, towards eight or nine in the morning. If the left was then required to move with this object at daybreak, it was necessary *to reiterate the order during the night*, as a verbal order, the execution of which was annulled by the very events of the previous night, could be very properly considered by the marshal as not to be carried out, with the very probable idea that the events would lead to new combinations the next day. Besides, to concentrate the somewhat scattered troops of the left, it was very necessary that d'Erlon's corps should receive orders before day. Everything, then, depends on knowing, what was said and done at the night conference.

3rd. As to the day of the 16th, the two orders expedited from

Charleroi, between seven and nine o'clock—one by Marshal Soult, the other by Napoleon himself—appear to have been, in fact, the first confirmation of the movement said to have been prescribed on the evening of the 15th. Both of these dispatches, seem to have preceded the reception of the information given by Grouchy, on the arrival of grand Prussian masses towards Ligny. What seems astonishing, is that an order, undoubtedly conceived by Napoleon towards six in the morning, should not have reached Frasne before eleven, and its execution not commenced till after midday.[5]

4th. It is then incontestable, that the whole time from five o'clock in the morning until noon, was not profited by in any suitable manner, and to my view, every one contributed somewhat to this blunder; because there was delay in the final resolution, and slowness in the transmission of orders, as well as in their execution.

5th. Be that as it may, at noon, the question entirely changed its aspect; he found himself in presence of 90,000 Prussians; the interest, wholly strategic, of the occupation of Quatre-Bras, then became but of secondary importance, compared with the tactical advantage of having Ney nearer to him, in hand, so as to have the power of at once casting one of his two corps of infantry and his heavy cavalry on the Prussians' right flank, which could be executed from Frasne as well as from Quatre-Bras. Undoubtedly, it had been desirable that this central point of Quatre-Bras, should be previously occupied by Reille's corps, and the light cavalry of Colbert and Lefèbre-Desnouettes; but this was no longer a decisive question, because, definitively, the route from Brussels could be covered by leaving these corps in front of Frasne, to mask that of the Prince of Orange, and nothing opposed the throwing of d'Erlon and Valmy on Bry, with 20,000 men, as became necessary when too late.

6th. This truth, that no enlightened military man will contest, proves that the non-occupation of Quatre-Bras on the 16th,

---

5. In order to admit all the accounts from St. Helena, and properly understand them, it would be necessary, 1st. That Marshal Ney had received the verbal order, urging him to advance on Quatre-Bras on the evening of the 15th; 2nd. That he had received anew the formal order during the night, that is, at the interview; 3rd. That he had at seven declared in his report, that he had again suspended its execution because of the junction of the two hostile armies; but the contents of the letters borne by Flahaut, or sent by Marshal Soult, really accord but slightly with this supposition.

though unfortunate, would not have had, in fact, the consequences attributed to it, *had orders been issued in time for the best possible employment of the left,* which was not done till three hours after midday.

This is, *Monsieur le Duc,* what seems to me to result, from all the minute investigations in which I have indulged. Consequently, I rest convinced, that if Marshal Ney received the verbal order of the evening of the 15th, and took upon himself to defer its execution, it was but a slight misfortune, very easily repaired the next morning. As to this day of the 16th June, I also believe that no blame should attach to him, *provided the formal injunction to advance at daybreak on Quatre-Bras, was not verbally reiterated in the night conference at Charleroi,* an uncertain thing, quite impossible to establish, if it be true that Marshal Soult was not present at the interview.[6]

Undoubtedly, Marshal Ney would have acted skilfully, by marching at all hazards on this important point, on the morning of the 16th; but a hesitation induced by a just prudence, and the non-execution of orders formally received, differ widely; and to blame this prudence, it would be necessary still to know, whether at the night conference, the emperor gave him to understand that he would send him further instructions at daybreak, a circumstance that would have shackled the marshal's movements.

In all that has preceded, I have admitted the existence of the verbal order of the evening of the 15th. If you succeed in demonstrating that the order written and borne by Flahaut, on the morning of the 16th, was the first and only one prescribing the occupation of Quatre-Bras, then the marshal would certainly be acquitted of all blame, and sheltered from all criticism. This frank and sincere expression will prove to you, to what extent I am disposed to render justice to your father, while preserving my impartiality as a historian.

This impartiality is, I trust, sufficiently well established, for anyone to dream of reproaching me with wishing to impair, in the slightest degree, the immense glory of Napoleon, as no one

---

6. The declaration of Marshal Soult, mentioned in your pamphlet, states that the emperor did not issue orders for the occupation of Quatre-Bras, till after breakfast on the 16th; but it does not positively deny, what may have been said verbally, and does not indicate that the major-general assisted at the night conference.

has proclaimed it louder than myself. A great captain may be induced, through false information, to make incorrect suppositions concerning the intentions of the enemy, and find himself led by it into committing actual faults, which would not be such had his suppositions been well founded. The emperor had, undoubtedly, powerful inducements for not taking a decisive course before three o'clock; and these were probably the same that determined him not to dispatch Flahaut till nine, to prescribe a movement which at that hour should have been already executed.

I have not considered it my duty to raise the charge made by many military men, on the marshal's recalling d'Erlon on the night of the 16th, though he perceived Reille's corps overwhelmed by superior forces: this was indeed an unfortunate incident, but most generals in his position would have undoubtedly acted in the same manner. Appreciating the importance of the route from Brussels to Charleroi, which was the line of the army's retreat, the marshal judged it necessary not to counterbalance, by a disaster at this point, the partial success the emperor might obtain at Ligny; such a resolution is of that number, that may not be opportune because of the turn of affairs, but which no enlightened military man would condemn.

Besides, on the next day—June 17th—the emperor only blamed him for having divided the left; he must have then wished, either that the two corps had come to Bry, or else had fought united at Quatre-Bras; now, as they were already engaged at the latter point, by his orders, how could Reille be withdrawn from the fight, and sent with d'Erlon upon Bry? It will, then, be objected, that it was not necessary to detach the latter alone. But we are well aware that he received, through Labédoyère, a direct order to march on Bry; a movement that would have certainly obtained an immense victory, had it been carried out.

I will terminate my long epistle with a few words on the battle of Waterloo, in which your father displayed such brilliant valour.

What has been said or printed, relative to the premature employment of cavalry, has appeared to me a puerile excuse; the real misfortune was, in not having it properly supported by infantry.

In my opinion, four principal causes led to this disaster:

The first, and most influential, was the arrival, skilfully combined, of Blucher, and the false movement that favoured this arrival;

The second, was the admirable firmness of the British infantry, joined to the *sang-froid* and *aplomb* of its chiefs;

The third, was the horrible weather, that had softened the ground, and rendered the offensive movements so toilsome, and retarded till one o'clock the attack that should have been made in the morning;

The fourth, was the inconceivable formation of the first corps, in masses very much too deep for the first grand attack.

The formation of masses, so unwieldy and so exposed to the ravages of the enemy's fire, was an incontestable error .... To whom should it be imputed? This will remain a problem for a long time to come.

Was it a mistake, caused by the double signification of the term *columns by divisions*, which applies indiscriminately, to the divisions of four regiments or to divisions of two platoons. A fatal confusion of terms, of which no one has yet dreamt of purging the military technology.

On the contrary, was it the intention of the chiefs of the French army, to form the troops in such a manner, that the divisions of four regiments should form but a single column? It would be interesting to know this, but it will no doubt ever remain a mystery.

However, these causes, as I have stated, were only secondary, and the most decisive was the arrival of Blucher with 65,000 Prussians, on the flank and rear of the French line; it was one of those events that human prudence cannot always avert.

You will perhaps find my letter full of repetitions, they were indispensable to give more clearness to my reasoning: as to my conclusions, if they are but eventual, it is, that far from pretending to be the judge, I should be borne on the list of simple reporters.

Accept the assurance of all my sentiments,

General J——

Paris, September 1st, 1841.

P. S. I send you here annexed, a printed copy of the letter I purpose adding, at the end of my *Political and Military Summary of*

1815. In attentively re-perusing this letter, I perceive that three essential observations have escaped me, and I think it my duty to notice them.

The first, tends to fortify the opinion, that Napoleon should not have attached any value to the isolated occupation of Quatre-Bras by the left wing, since the right could not press on as far as Sombref. In fact, it is evident that if the two points were occupied simultaneously, the position then offered the most brilliant advantages, united to perfect security, because the right would be covered from the English, while the left remained without the slightest uneasiness from the Prussians, who could no longer reach it through Sombref. Thus the two masses of the army not only reciprocally supported each other, but were free from all anxiety of being taken in flank or in rear, and had, besides, a reserve of 40,000 of the elite to march in the intermediate space, and support both.

On the contrary, let us suppose the left of these masses pushed alone on Quatre-Bras, Sombref not being strongly occupied; then this body would be in manifest danger, thus venturing between two great armies, as it might be assailed on all sides; from Brussels by the English, from Nivelles by the Belgians, and from Sombref by the whole Prussian army.

It would be the same with the right wing, if pushed, on the evening of the 15th, as far as Sombref, the left not occupying Quatre-Bras. It is thus incontestable, that the simultaneous occupation of the two points was necessary, in order to constitute a skilful manoeuvre, and prove important in its results.

Another reflection has occurred to me, relative to the orders of the 15th June: it is, that on that day, Marshal Grouchy commanded only the cavalry reserves, and had not an infantry soldier at his disposal, as it was only on the morning of the 16th, that the command of the right wing was conferred upon him. It could, then, be very possible, that Napoleon had ordered the chief of his cavalry to press forward with his numerous squadrons to Sombref, not in order to take up a position for battle, but solely as a strong reconnoitering party, with the double object of gathering reliable information, and annoying the movements of the allies, while concentrating their forces by this crossroad. Then on the morning of the 16th, the two masses of infantry should have been required to occupy, militarily and simultaneously, the two decisive points of the whole operation, thus rendering the junction of the enemy's armies impossible.

This circumstance of the cavalry command, to which I have not given sufficient attention, world authorize us in believing, that Napoleon might order Grouchy, during the 15th, to press forward to Sombref, without dreaming of advancing infantry masses separately on Quatre-Bras. The encumbrances existing at the different bridges on the Sambre, and the delays experienced by the infantry, still strengthen this opinion. Besides, I believe I have demonstrated, that it was more prudent, and at the same time sufficient, to take possession of Quatre-Bras on the morning of the 16th.

The last observation I think it proper to make, relates to the resolution taken by General Reille, not to put his corps on the march at ten o'clock on the morning of the 16th, after General Flahaut had communicated to him the orders he was bearing to Marshal Ney. I do not think, that he is deserving of the least censure on this account: we must not forget, that General Reille had just sent—nine o'clock—the positive information of the presence of the entire Prussian army towards Ligny: he must have concluded from this, that the left would be called upon to take part in the attack of this army, and that it would be unfortunate if, after such information, he took the Genape route, when it would be necessary to turn to the right towards Bry.

This reasoning was more than logical, it was based on the laws of *la grande tactique*, and the emperor himself, had he been present at Gosselies, at the reception of the information given by General Girard, would not have acted differently from Reille. We must also add, that the emperor's orders were addressed to Marshal Ney, and that it was from him that he should expect the final decision, as to the movement to be made.

However, this delay had little influence on the course of affairs; nothing would have resulted from it, except at the commencement of the battle of Quatre-Bras, between two and four o'clock. If Reille, followed later by d'Erlon had reached this point at midday, it is probable that the Prince of Orange would have been dislodged, before the arrival of Wellington, and of the English coming from Brussels and Nivelles: Marshal Ney, instead of being repulsed and forced to retreat on Frasne?, would have maintained his position, but this was all that could be expected from him, as towards evening he would have had over 40,000 men against him.

He could not have even held this post, but under the supposition that d'Erlon had been with him; so that this would not have given one man the more, to fight the Prussians: the marshal would have repulsed Wellington, instead of being repulsed by him—that is all.

The battle of Ligny could not then have produced decisive results, but with the co-operation of the whole or half of the left wing; and to effect this, the surest means were to do what was undoubtedly Reille's wish: to halt the left in rear of the rivulet of Pont-à-Miqueloup, between Gosselies and Frasne, in order to detach from it a strong portion upon Bry, on the Prussian flank.

I think, *Monsieur le Duc*, that all learned military men will up hold me in my opinion.

Accept the renewed expressions of all my sentiments,

General J——

Paris, October 18th, 1841.

ALSO FROM LEONAUR
AVAILABLE IN SOFTCOVER OR HARDCOVER WITH DUST JACKET

IRON TIMES WITH THE GUARDS *by An O. E. (G. P. A. Fildes)*—The Experiences of an Officer of the Coldstream Guards on the Western Front During the First World War.

THE GREAT WAR IN THE MIDDLE EAST: 1 *by W. T. Massey*—The Desert Campaigns & How Jerusalem Was Won---two classic accounts in one volume.

THE GREAT WAR IN THE MIDDLE EAST: 2 *by W. T. Massey*—Allenby's Final Triumph.

SMITH-DORRIEN *by Horace Smith-Dorrien*—Isandlwhana to the Great War.

1914 *by Sir John French*—The Early Campaigns of the Great War by the British Commander.

GRENADIER *by E. R. M. Fryer*—The Recollections of an Officer of the Grenadier Guards throughout the Great War on the Western Front.

BATTLE, CAPTURE & ESCAPE *by George Pearson*—The Experiences of a Canadian Light Infantryman During the Great War.

DIGGERS AT WAR *by R. Hugh Knyvett & G. P. Cuttriss*—"Over There" With the Australians by R. Hugh Knyvett and Over the Top With the Third Australian Division by G. P. Cuttriss. Accounts of Australians During the Great War in the Middle East, at Gallipoli and on the Western Front.

HEAVY FIGHTING BEFORE US *by George Brenton Laurie*—The Letters of an Officer of the Royal Irish Rifles on the Western Front During the Great War.

THE CAMELIERS *by Oliver Hogue*—A Classic Account of the Australians of the Imperial Camel Corps During the First World War in the Middle East.

RED DUST *by Donald Black*—A Classic Account of Australian Light Horsemen in Palestine During the First World War.

THE LEAN, BROWN MEN *by Angus Buchanan*—Experiences in East Africa During the Great War with the 25th Royal Fusiliers—the Legion of Frontiersmen.

THE NIGERIAN REGIMENT IN EAST AFRICA *by W. D. Downes*—On Campaign During the Great War 1916-1918.

THE 'DIE-HARDS' IN SIBERIA *by John Ward*—With the Middlesex Regiment Against the Bolsheviks 1918-19.

AVAILABLE ONLINE AT **www.leonaur.com**
AND FROM ALL GOOD BOOK STORES

ALSO FROM LEONAUR
AVAILABLE IN SOFTCOVER OR HARDCOVER WITH DUST JACKET

FARAWAY CAMPAIGN *by F. James*—Experiences of an Indian Army Cavalry Officer in Persia & Russia During the Great War.

REVOLT IN THE DESERT *by T. E. Lawrence*—An account of the experiences of one remarkable British officer's war from his own perspective.

MACHINE-GUN SQUADRON *by A. M. G.*—The 20th Machine Gunners from British Yeomanry Regiments in the Middle East Campaign of the First World War.

A GUNNER'S CRUSADE *by Antony Bluett*—The Campaign in the Desert, Palestine & Syria as Experienced by the Honourable Artillery Company During the Great War.

DESPATCH RIDER *by W. H. L. Watson*—The Experiences of a British Army Motorcycle Despatch Rider During the Opening Battles of the Great War in Europe.

TIGERS ALONG THE TIGRIS *by E. J. Thompson*—The Leicestershire Regiment in Mesopotamia During the First World War.

HEARTS & DRAGONS *by Charles R. M. F. Crutwell*—The 4th Royal Berkshire Regiment in France and Italy During the Great War, 1914-1918.

INFANTRY BRIGADE: 1914 *by John Ward*—The Diary of a Commander of the 15th Infantry Brigade, 5th Division, British Army, During the Retreat from Mons.

DOING OUR 'BIT' *by Ian Hay*—Two Classic Accounts of the Men of Kitchener's 'New Army' During the Great War including *The First 100,000 & All In It*.

AN EYE IN THE STORM *by Arthur Ruhl*—An American War Correspondent's Experiences of the First World War from the Western Front to Gallipoli-and Beyond.

STAND & FALL *by Joe Cassells*—With the Middlesex Regiment Against the Bolsheviks 1918-19.

RIFLEMAN MACGILL'S WAR *by Patrick MacGill*—A Soldier of the London Irish During the Great War in Europe including *The Amateur Army, The Red Horizon & The Great Push*.

WITH THE GUNS *by C. A. Rose & Hugh Dalton*—Two First Hand Accounts of British Gunners at War in Europe During World War 1- Three Years in France with the Guns and With the British Guns in Italy.

THE BUSH WAR DOCTOR *by Robert V. Dolbey*—The Experiences of a British Army Doctor During the East African Campaign of the First World War.

AVAILABLE ONLINE AT www.leonaur.com
AND FROM ALL GOOD BOOK STORES

ALSO FROM LEONAUR
AVAILABLE IN SOFTCOVER OR HARDCOVER WITH DUST JACKET

THE 9TH—THE KING'S (LIVERPOOL REGIMENT) IN THE GREAT WAR 1914 - 1918 *by Enos H. G. Roberts*—Mersey to mud—war and Liverpool men.

THE GAMBARDIER *by Mark Severn*—The experiences of a battery of Heavy artillery on the Western Front during the First World War.

FROM MESSINES TO THIRD YPRES *by Thomas Floyd*—A personal account of the First World War on the Western front by a 2/5th Lancashire Fusilier.

THE IRISH GUARDS IN THE GREAT WAR - VOLUME 1 *by Rudyard Kipling*—Edited and Compiled from Their Diaries and Papers—The First Battalion.

THE IRISH GUARDS IN THE GREAT WAR - VOLUME 1 *by Rudyard Kipling*—Edited and Compiled from Their Diaries and Papers—The Second Battalion.

ARMOURED CARS IN EDEN *by K. Roosevelt*—An American President's son serving in Rolls Royce armoured cars with the British in Mesopatamia & with the American Artillery in France during the First World War.

CHASSEUR OF 1914 *by Marcel Dupont*—Experiences of the twilight of the French Light Cavalry by a young officer during the early battles of the great war in Europe.

TROOP HORSE & TRENCH *by R.A. Lloyd*—The experiences of a British Lifeguardsman of the household cavalry fighting on the western front during the First World War 1914-18.

THE EAST AFRICAN MOUNTED RIFLES *by C.J. Wilson*—Experiences of the campaign in the East African bush during the First World War.

THE LONG PATROL *by George Berrie*—A Novel of Light Horsemen from Gallipoli to the Palestine campaign of the First World War.

THE FIGHTING CAMELIERS *by Frank Reid*—The exploits of the Imperial Camel Corps in the desert and Palestine campaigns of the First World War.

STEEL CHARIOTS IN THE DESERT *by S. C. Rolls*—The first world war experiences of a Rolls Royce armoured car driver with the Duke of Westminster in Libya and in Arabia with T.E. Lawrence.

WITH THE IMPERIAL CAMEL CORPS IN THE GREAT WAR *by Geoffrey Inchbald*—The story of a serving officer with the British 2nd battalion against the Senussi and during the Palestine campaign.

AVAILABLE ONLINE AT **www.leonaur.com**
AND FROM ALL GOOD BOOK STORES